tea & thread:

portraits of middle eastern women far from home

Sally Bathgate
Katrina Flett Gulbrandsen

To the women whose stories are the heart of this book:

Our deepest thanks to each of you for your willingness to open your lives to us and speak with us about your experiences. We grieve for your losses and for the difficult circumstances that led to our meeting. Thank you for making us welcome. We wish for you to be as warmly welcomed wherever you may go. We wish you peace in your lives and peace for your homelands. You will remain in our thoughts and prayers always.

God bless you.

إهداء

إلى السيدات اللاتي شاركن بقصصهن في هذا الكتاب نهدي شكرنا الجزيل لكل منهن على فتح قلوبهن و مشاركتهن و إدلائهن بالشهادة و الاختبارات الحية التي عاشتها كل منهن.

إننا نشترك معكن في الحزن من أجل فقدان الأحباء، و كذلك الظروف الرهيبة التي عاشتها كل منكن و التي سمعناها منكن خلال لقائنا معاً.

نود أن نقدم لكم الشكر الجزيل على ترحيبكم بنا و نتمنى لكم أن تنلن نفس الترحيب في أي مكان تذهبن إليه. نصلي أن يعم سلام الرب حياتكن و أوطانكن و نود أن نخبركم بأنكم ستظلون دائماً في قلوبنا و أفكارنا و صلواتنا.

ليبارك الرب حياتكن.

Marketing & Public Relations Director
Sally Bathgate

Creative Director
Katrina Flett Gulbrandsen

Editor
Alissa Herbaly Coons

Graphic Designer
Rebecca Derkenne

Lead Photographer
Katrina Flett Gulbrandsen

Recipe Coordinator
Sally Bathgate

Handicraft Coordinator
Katrina Flett Gulbrandsen

Publisher

Grace Abounding Books

tea & thread:
portraits of middle eastern women
far from home

Published in Australia by
Grace Abounding Books,
an imprint of Anglican Aid.

anglicanaid.org.au

[ISBN 9780646972831]

Contributors

A heartfelt thank you to each of our contributors and volunteers for the work you have done on behalf of each person who shares a story, craft, or recipe in this collection. Without your compassion, generosity, time, and talents, this project would not have been possible. It has been a privilege to work with all of you, and though many seas separate us, our moments together have yielded this book. Each of you has brought something unique and crucial to tea & thread, and for that we are so thankful.

Thank you also to our 121 crowdfunding donors! Your interest and investment has been essential to the life of this project. Our sincere thanks as well to Anglican Aid for providing a home for this book, offering support for everything from publishing assistance through to fundraising administration. We send our gratitude especially to Eddie Ozols, Michelle Chase, and Dianne Davies.

Editorial assistance
Leah Moore-Evans
Katrina Flett Gulbrandsen
Lucy Larkins
Natalie Swann
Helen Bathgate

Handcrafting
Kelly Fowler
Heather King
Faisal Afghani
Faatima
Menahi Khoury
Halah Al-Far
Wendy Flett
Hasan Kan'an
Kaia Ireson

Illustration
Matthew Baker
Leah Sands

Recipe testers
Sally Bathgate
Elizabeth Schandelmeier Gilgunn
Maya Henry
Alissa Herbaly Coons

Translation/interpreting
Nicole Lavezzari
Stephen
Tala Qarrain
Hadeel Qumhiya
Ayat Um Majid
Samar Al-far
George Rouchdi
Ashraf Youssef
Karam Awad

Photographic
Wilma Steenbeek
Sophie Timothy
Claire Norton
Stian Gulbrandsen
Kelly Fowler
Taryn Lammi
Alissa Herbaly Coons
Rebecca Derkenne
Ben Bathgate

Personal thanks to
Ben Bathgate
Rasha Ahmad
Lana Haddad
Maha Micho
Stian Gulbrandsen
Fatima Mardenli
Maryam Khan
Hind
Leah Moore-Evans
Erzsébet Árkus

Writers

Katrina Flett Gulbrandsen
Katrina is originally from New South Wales, Australia. She recently spent two years living in Jordan with her family, studying Arabic and working as a Program Development Officer for World Relief Germany-Jordan. She is a student in the Master of Religion in Middle Eastern and North African Studies program at the Institute of Middle East Studies, Lebanon. Katrina lives in Norway.

Sally Bathgate
Sally is from Sydney, Australia. She and her family spent three years in Amman, Jordan, studying Arabic and immersing themselves in Middle Eastern culture. Prior to this, Sally worked for three-and-a-half years amongst the predominantly Arab migrant community in Western Sydney with the Anglican church. She is now based in Sydney.

Nicole Lavezzari
Nicole and her family lived and studied Arabic in Syria for three years before being forced to leave due to the current conflict. They now live and work with Syrian refugees in a neighbouring country. Nicole is a nurse and the founder and director of a small non-profit handicraft cooperative that provides Syrian refugee women with financial and psycho-social support.

Taryn Lammi
Taryn was born in the USA but grew up in Turkey. After completing high school she travelled to the Middle East to do volunteer work with Syrian refugees for six months. In the Middle East, she interviewed Syrian refugee women and recorded their stories. She now studies Journalism at Liberty University, Lynchburg, Virginia.

Kelly Fowler
Kelly is originally from California, USA. She is a nurse practitioner and has lived and worked in Jordan for six years. She has a keen interest in the local herbs and natural skin care remedies of the region. She lives with her husband and two young boys and has a great love of patchwork Bedouin tents and smoky tea.

Jonathan Morgan
Jonathan and his wife studied Arabic and lived in Amman, Jordan, for two years. During his recent immersion, he worked with the non-governmental organisation (NGO) Hope and Trust, providing practical assistance to asylum seekers and refugees. Originally from Wales, he is currently living in Sweden, working on his Master's degree in Middle Eastern Studies at Lund University.

About tea & thread

Tea is synonymous with hospitality in the Middle Eastern world, and although the ritual may vary from place to place, the meaning is the same, *Ahlan wa sahlan* — Welcome, you are amongst family, may it go well with you!

On behalf of all of the volunteers who have made this book possible, let me welcome you to a glimpse into the lives of women from the Middle East. In the course of my recent experiences in Jordan with refugee women and their families, I worked and lived among a fascinating flow of people. My memories of these encounters form an ever-shifting collage of vibrant parties, wild children, miscommunication, heavily-lined eyes, anxiety, patterned mattresses in bare rooms, different opinions, the scent and gentle bubbling of the water-pipe, times of inclusion and exclusion, my scarf routinely falling off my head, the call to prayer, so much food, and always tea.

The tea & thread project is a tribute to all of the women who have shared a cup of tea with me and the other contributors, and the relationships that have grown from this hospitality. We met in so many situations, each of our personalities and perspectives uniquely shaped and evolving, inextricably linked to our culture, religion, education, and upbringing. For those far from home to whom this book is dedicated, their experiences have also been shaped by the violence and instability of war; but this is not their whole story.

The stories included in the book offer glimpses into memories of life before the war, war-time difficulties, and the uncertainties of being a refugee. These glimpses are presented through the filter of translation, through the fragmentation of trauma, and through the limits of time and what can be put into words.

At times working on this collection, it has seemed absurd to write about deeply traumatic events and then move on to the seemingly trivial details of craft instructions or cookery. But these seeming trivialities are actually a form of intangible wealth — they are the stuff of precious ordinary life. It is often a comfort and source of healing to remember and recreate sensory memories that recall happier times; even in the midst of tragedy and upheaval, people continue to need to eat and to keep their hands busy.

To be a refugee is to be uprooted in one moment in life. It is, or ought to be, a temporary condition. We wish for each woman who has offered her story here to have hope for a better future, where she is known and appreciated, secure and at peace. Because of the vulnerabilities of these women and their families, in consultation with them, we have taken some measures to protect their privacy.

Over many cups of tea, despite our differences, the participants in this project have strengthened the thread of our shared humanity. We would like to extend this thread to you, our readers. We hope that these stories will kindle your openness to refugees and new immigrant families in your own communities; that you will be encouraged to take action — to offer hospitality, to listen, to include, and to start new conversations and connections.

Thank you for supporting the tea & thread project! All of the profits from sales of the book will go to further the work of humanitarian relief projects working with refugees in the Middle East.

Allah makum — God be with you all!

Katrina

About our recipes

As my family prepared to leave for our three years in the Middle East, we were given a Middle Eastern cookbook by one of our church friends, George. It turned out that this comprehensive tome was written by his mother, Tess Mallos, who was well-known in Australia for her Middle Eastern cookery.

Her book, *The Complete Middle Eastern Cook Book*, is stunning. My own copy is now well used — I lugged it half way around the world and back. And it accompanied me on many a visit to new friends in the Middle East.

In my adopted home the book was useful in two ways: firstly, as a tool for learning the Arabic language — talking about food is concrete, repetitive, and contained. My friends and I could easily navigate the topic of food and cookery with my broken Arabic and their limited English. Secondly, the book was a bridge between cultures. I found that the simplest way to connect with someone was to show an interest in their food.

I cannot express the joy it brought to the women I met when I enjoyed their cooking and shared a meal with them. To them, being visited and being able to show hospitality brought blessing upon them — and even more so for those displaced, where all semblance of normality had been violently ripped away. Somehow, serving a stranger in their own home restored their own dignity and humanity.

Many of these women were more than willing to share and to teach. Recipes are not usually written down, but learned through following the hands-on instruction of a loved one: mother, grandmother, aunt. We have done our best to write these recipes in a way that will be more familiar to our readers. Be aware that there is a wide variety of methods and ingredients used for any particular dish, so you may make a friend who disagrees entirely with how we've presented a recipe!

I did have one friend who refused to share her recipes with me. She was insistent that if I wanted to eat what she made, I must visit her and eat it with her! Such is the heart of Middle Eastern hospitality — generous, abundant, sacrificial, and very persistent.

It was this heart of hospitality — and from some of the poorest people I've met — that was a great personal challenge to me living in the Middle East. I naturally have a tendency to frugality, efficiency, and conservation of time, money, and energy. This is a product of some of my Western values, but also a product of laziness and apathy, if I'm honest. But these women have inspired me to open my home, make sacrifices of my time and money, and pursue a new kind of love — using the abundance of my home comforts for others.

I hope this heart of hospitality overflows in the pages of this book. I suspect that there are many of us who can learn from these women how to love others in our homes and through our families, even in the midst of great suffering.

Saha — to your health!

Sally

Foreword

There is nothing quite like food or craft for bringing women together. Whatever their backgrounds, it seems to be the same all around the world. Time spent alongside each other in the preparation of food, or working on a creative project, slows us down a little from the rush of normal life, allowing easy sharing and openness from which real friendships are formed. This wonderful collection of stories and recipes bears eloquent testimony to the natural bonding of women over food, drink, and craft — tea and thread. As readers, we are invited into the hospitality that is the core of this book, which began in a variety of cross-cultural relationships among refugee women, aid workers, volunteers, and friends. Many of the stories come from refugee craft initiatives, where women meet to encourage each other and maintain their resilience in the face of the severe hardship of losing so much that was familiar to them.

In the following pages you will meet some of these women, as well as other Middle Eastern women of varying religious and cultural heritages. These stories are often sad and, for us reading them in the safety of Australia, it is difficult to comprehend the horror that so many of these women and their families have had to endure. However, it is deeply important for us to listen to each woman who has offered her story here — both to understand the human cost of the wars that have devastated their homelands, and to increase our compassion. Despite their many losses, the women in this book share with us some of the cultural riches that remain in their keep: favourite family recipes, as well as instructions for the best soap in the world, olive oil soap, from an ancient recipe handed down from mother to daughter over the centuries in the Levant.

I trust this collection will find a place on your table, where it will inspire your own practice of hospitality.

On behalf of Anglican Aid,

Dianne Davies

Foreground: mosque in the desert. In the distance: Zaatari refugee camp, population 79,000, on the outskirts of the village of Zaatari. A total of 733,210 people of concern were registered with UNHCR in Jordan as of March 2017, including 657,621 Syrians, 62,445 Iraqis and 13,144 others. Across Jordan, those numbers mean 89 refugees per 1000 inhabitants, but villages like Zaatari bear a much heavier burden. In addition to the presence of the camp, the population in the village has doubled from 10,000 to 20,000 with the influx of refugees [figures: UNHCR and Mercy Corps].

The Middle Eastern refugee crisis

According to the United Nations High Commissioner for Refugees (UNHCR),

"[In 2016-2017] The situation in the Middle East and North Africa region remains complex and volatile, with multiple conflicts triggering massive levels of displacement... political solutions to the conflicts remain elusive...

"The Syrian crisis has continued to take a severe toll on the Middle East and North Africa region, with 6.1 million Internally Displaced Persons and over 4.8 million refugees in the neighbouring countries of Egypt, Iraq, Jordan, Lebanon and Turkey...

"While countries neighbouring Syria remain at the forefront of the crisis, hosting a large majority of this population, their generosity has put increasing strain on national infrastructure, making it increasingly difficult for refugees to access basic services... Many have exhausted their savings and are sinking further into poverty. In Lebanon, 70 per cent of refugee households currently live below the poverty line, with more than 52 per cent living in extreme poverty. In Jordan, 90 per cent of the 513,000 registered Syrian refugees living in urban areas are [living] below the national poverty line... Consequently, the number of Syrians seeking refuge beyond the Middle East and North Africa region has risen...

"Instability and displacement also continue in Iraq, Libya and Yemen... Since January 2014, the escalating violence in Iraq has led to the internal displacement of more than 3.3 million people. Humanitarian partners estimate that more than 10 million Iraqis currently require some form of humanitarian assistance. While Turkey continues to host more than half of the over 230,000 registered Iraqi refugees in the region, 2016 has seen hundreds of thousands of Iraqis take to the sea in an attempt to reach safety in Europe...

"With resettlement needs continuing to rise globally in light of the increasing numbers of refugees and growing vulnerabilities, the UNHCR will continue advocating for increased resettlement capacity [globally]..."

[excerpted from the UNHCR Global Appeal 2017 Update - Middle East and North Africa (MENA) regional summary, www.unhcr.org]

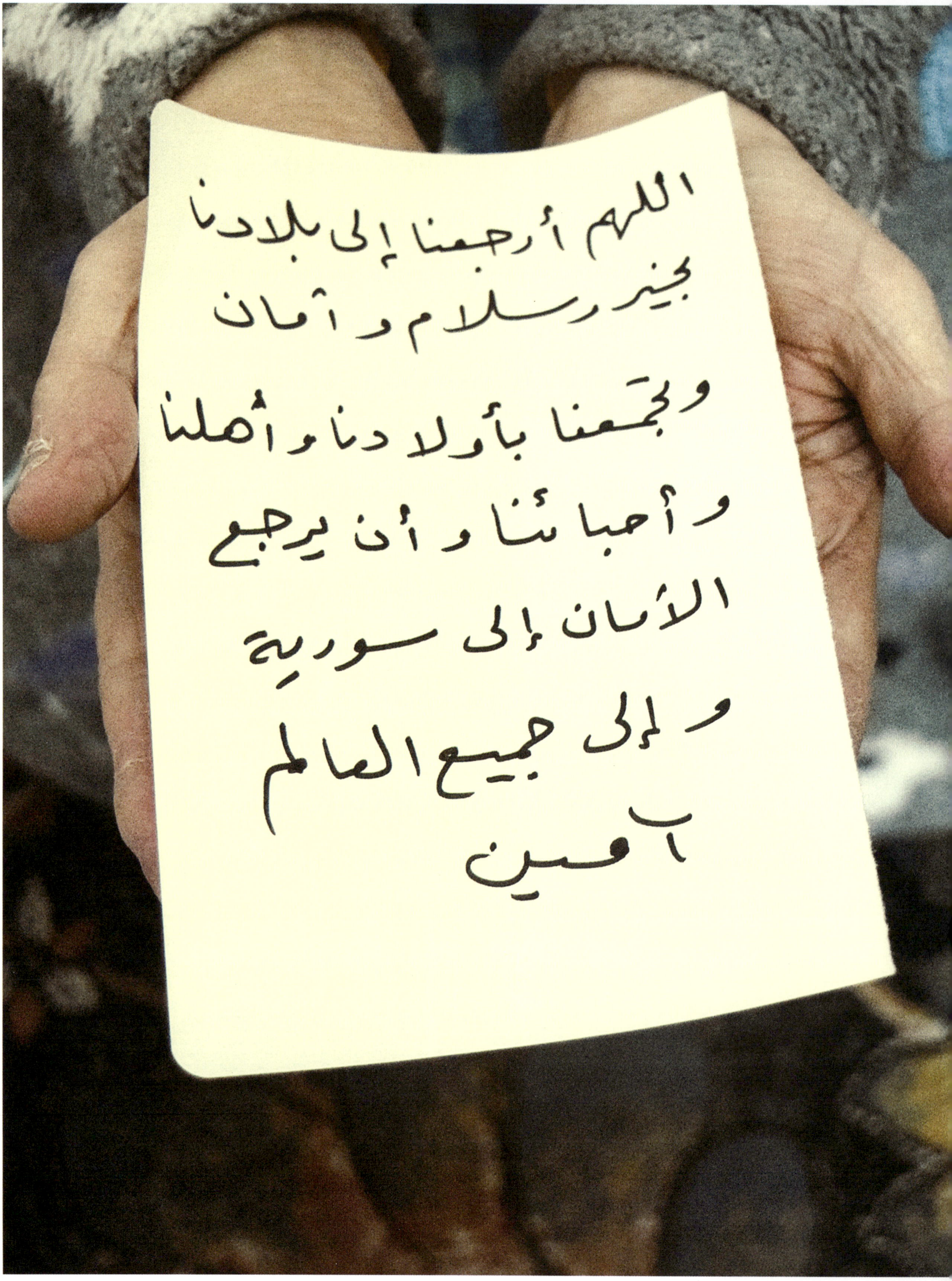

اللهم أرجعنا إلى بلادنا
بخير وسلام و أمان
وتجمعنا بأولادنا و أهلنا
و أحبائنا و أن يرجع
الأمان إلى سورية
و إلى جميع العالم
آمين

O God, bring us back to our country
in wellness and peace and safety.
May you reunite us with our children,
our parents, and all our loved ones.
May you restore peace
to Syria and to the whole world.

Amen

Contents

RINDA home: Syria
far from home since March 2012

رندا

STORY TARYN LAMMI | **PHOTOGRAPHY** TARYN LAMMI AND KATRINA FLETT GULBRANDSEN

"No matter what, you must keep walking. Do not go looking for me, and do not stop."

The atmosphere in the family room was charged with contrasting emotions. Six joyous children threaded in and out of the room. An Indian soap opera blared its melodrama from the television. The children's mother, Rinda, cried as she recalled the night her family escaped from Syria into Jordan, on foot.

Rinda spoke, "There were around one thousand adults and just as many children. We were surrounded on all sides by mountains. It was cold and the night was pitch black. My body shook with adrenaline. I was not doing well; it felt like the ground beneath me was moving. I could not carry my children, so I used an extra headscarf to tie together their hands to try to keep them together. As I did this, I told them, 'No matter what, you must keep walking. Do not go looking for me, and do not stop.' I was terrified of losing my children in the blackness.

"Before we began our night journey to the border, we were given sleeping pills to give to the younger children to silence them. We were told, 'You all must be like a herd; stay together!'

"At one point in the journey, I realised I had fallen behind. I couldn't see anyone in front of me or behind me. I was trembling. All kinds of scenarios raced through my mind. My chest hurt, and I was exhausted. I stopped. Where was everyone? Suddenly, the voice of a man spoke to me and asked, 'Why have you stopped?' I couldn't see anything. 'I'm from the Free Syrian Army,' the man said. 'I'm here to help you. Keep walking; there are other people ahead.'

I was so tired that the man took my struggling child, with the promise he would take care of her and bring her safely to my husband. Once he took her, I heard two women behind me saying, in hushed voices, 'We're here too.' It comforted me.

"Finally, I arrived at the meeting place and was able to find my husband and the rest of my family. I searched for my young daughter's face amongst them. It was not there. 'Where is our daughter?' my husband asked. 'I gave her to a man who said he was with the Free Syrian Army,' I answered. 'But what if he wasn't? It's dark; you couldn't see a thing!' I was panicking, 'What was I supposed to do? I needed help. I couldn't carry her!'

"My husband frantically and desperately began looking around. After a time, some people found her and brought her to us. My husband wept with relief.

"From there, we continued our journey across the border into Jordan. My husband would not let go of any of us. He had two of our daughters in his arms and was also holding on to me. As soon as we crossed the border, there were Jordanians waiting there to help us. They gave us water to drink and let us wash our faces.

"Regardless of the warm welcome and relief, I felt my heart was being ripped out of my chest — I knew I could never return to Syria. We had just left a land full of fear and entered into a new land filled with the sorrows of many other Syrians."

LUBYI AU BAMYA MA BANDOURA WA TOUM

(beans or okra in tomato & garlic sauce)

Bamya is a favourite in Rinda's family. During *Ramadan*, she buys heaps of okra from the *souk*, and makes up a big pot to serve for *Iftar* meals. She admits that it usually only lasts for a couple of days!

Serves: 4 - 6

INGREDIENTS:

500g (1 lb 2 oz) green beans/okra

125ml (4 fl oz or ½ cup) vinegar

60ml (2 fl oz or ¼ cup) olive oil

200g (7 oz) minced meat (lamb or beef)

2 garlic cloves, chopped

1 400g (12 fl oz) can diced tomato

1 tablespoon pomegranate molasses*

salt and freshly ground black pepper, to taste

2 tablespoons chopped flat-leaf parsley

METHOD:

OKRA PREP: Wash the okra well, handling gently. Trim the stem end without cutting the pod. Remove any fuzz by rubbing the okra gently with a nylon scourer, under running water. Dry well with a paper towel or cloth. Place into a bowl with the vinegar. Toss to coat and leave for 30 minutes. Drain, rinse and dry well.

BEAN PREP: Soak beans to wash well. Top and tail beans, and cut into 5cm (2-inch) lengths.

Fry the beans/okra quickly in the oil. Remove from the frying pan with a slotted spoon.

Fry the minced meat and garlic until the meat is brown, then add the canned tomato, salt and pepper, and pomegranate molasses. Cover and simmer for 15 minutes. Stir in the beans/okra and parsley. Cover and simmer for a further 15 - 20 minutes, or until the beans/okra are tender.

Serve hot or lukewarm in the traditional way, with flatbread. The beans are also very good served chilled.

Note: Tinned or frozen okra may be used. In this case, skip the frying step.

*You can replace pomegranate molasses with 1 tablespoon tomato paste and 1 teaspoon sugar.

SUPER GAME

Detailed Syrian Arabesque work waits to be repaired in an antique shop, Jerash, Jordan.

UNHCR
The UN

Zaatari refugee camp, which covers 5.3 km^2, provides shelter to more than 79,000 Syrian refugees near the Syrian border in Jordan. Since its establishment in July, 2012, the camp has housed more than 460,000 individuals, with a peak population of more than 200,000 residents in April, 2013 [figures: UNHCR].

SAMAR
home: Homs, Syria
far from home since 2013

سمر

STORY & PHOTOGRAPHY KATRINA FLETT GULBRANDSEN

"I always try to make them feel that tomorrow will be more beautiful, and that it won't rain forever. There will come a day when our lives will change for the better. Aye, I always tell them, 'bukra ahla' — tomorrow is a better day."

Samar sat opposite me in my small stone-tiled kitchen, expertly slicing through a bunch of fragrant, flat-leaf parsley. The space we shared was intimate, quiet. We were both strangers there, in that dusty desert town. We sat so close to the border of her country, yet her home remained impossibly distant.

As we sliced herbs and slowly filled the bowl, we chatted in very basic Arabic. Samar was so patient with me as I searched for words to ask about her life. She spoke of Syria, her home, her family, her farm, her history. Then, a melody escaped her lips, "an old song of Syria", she said. The sound of her singing was haunting, a lyrical expression imbued with deep loss and grief.

She told me how, as a child, she loved to sit under the old Persian walnut tree at the family farm. Her family grew olives and grapes, and tended a bountiful fruit orchard much loved by her mother. Her mother took care of her ten children and made wonderful meals from their farm produce.

"My mother and father had a very special relationship," Samar said. "My father loved my mother so much that he put all the family property under her name, to show his respect for her. As children, we never saw them fight or heard them speak badly of each other."

We lingered over her treasured pictures. They showed a young girl with flowing dark hair posing with full-blossomed rose bushes, standing under tall pine trees, reclining in olive groves. "I was brought up like a princess," she said.

"Weekdays we would spend in our village house, attending school with other students, some *Sunni, Shia, Alawite* and Christian. I had many friends, and felt safe and secure." She pulled out another photograph showing Muslim and Christian teenagers, clad in denim overalls, with linked arms and self-conscious smiles. And then another taken some years later, the denim long gone — a serious-looking young woman in boldly coloured satin and sequins, big sleeves and big makeup... a coming of age story unfolding in the tattered prints.

We reached her wedding photo. Samar told me, "I was married on the 24th of June, 1998, in Homs. My husband was an engineer in Syria. He worked very hard and we acquired property and wealth. We had four children; the eldest is now sixteen and the youngest nine years old."

"One day, at the start of the war, we were warned by an *Alawite* neighbour not to return to our family farm. While we were safe in the village, our property was raided and our beautiful farm was burnt to the ground. Thanks to God, we were safe — but we couldn't go back. We moved to a safer area. My husband returned to Homs to work every day until it became too unsafe on the roads. I was so scared for him. One day we decided that we were risking too much; we had to get out of the country. We used the money we had saved and came to Jordan.

"We survive in Jordan below the poverty line, living from day to day on support from humanitarian organisations. It is illegal and dangerous for us to work. Many people have been sent back to Syria for working."

"Our biggest concern is for our children; they are suffering. In Syria, they were A-grade students. Here the schools are understaffed and overcrowded. We can't afford better schools, extra tuition, or to send our son to university. What future can we offer them if we stay here? They have been forced to grow up so quickly; they seem to carry the weight of the world on their shoulders. I wish my childhood for my children. I always tell them, *'bukra ahla'* — tomorrow is a better day. It is hard to give them hope, when I feel so little myself. How do I motivate them and keep them positive?

"From the start, my husband was against attempting the dangerous route through Turkey and into Europe. But we couldn't wait any longer. He said, 'I either go and die at sea, or I find a way like those who did before me.' We agreed that we wouldn't risk the children's safety, and decided that my husband would make the journey alone. I was terrified of what this could mean for all of us.

"I didn't sleep for two nights, waiting to hear if he had crossed the sea safely to Greece. Thanks to God, the phone finally rang! He tried to call regularly as he travelled through Europe on his way to Germany. He was welcomed warmly in some countries, and chased and threatened in others. The journey was tough, and he didn't like to talk in detail about his ordeal. After some weeks he made it to a reception centre in Germany and applied for asylum.

"He calls us sometimes up to three or four times a day! I try to keep brave for him and the kids, but I am so fearful and stressed. I am alone. I am now mother and father, and the future is so uncertain. I try to give my family hope. I tell my children, 'It won't be long before we see your father again,' but to be honest, I have this feeling that we might never see him again. I try to encourage my husband, I say, 'You have taken a great risk for the kids, you have to be patient and bear our separation a little longer; we agreed to take this risk, and we shall accept the consequences.'

"I'm tired," Samar told me, "so tired. I need my husband. My kids need their father."

She waited for the call, for the permission to be reunited with him in Germany. She waited for a year.

My phone beeps. They have arrived! Next comes a photo of her children playing in a German town square, then one of her sitting on a park bench, surrounded by golden-leafed trees and fog. A husband and wife stand formally, reunited, and then, her daughter smiling, standing by a lake filled with white swans.

I exhale and my tears start to well. I let out an *Alhamdulillah* — Praise be to God, the sun has come out, tomorrow has come!

TABBOULEH

(burghul and parsley salad)

"Come over," Samar says. "I will make *tabbouleh*!" This cold grain salad is a staple across the Middle East. It can accompany any dish, or it can be eaten on its own by the bowlful!

Serves: 6 - 8 (as a side)

INGREDIENTS:

150g (5 oz or ¾ cup) burghul (also known as bulgur or cracked wheat), with 250ml (9 fl oz or 1 cup) water to soak

2 large bunches flat-leaf parsley, washed well

60g (2 oz or ½ cup) finely chopped spring onions (scallions)

1 bunch mint, leaves finely chopped

4 Lebanese cucumbers, finely diced

60ml (2 fl oz or ¼ cup) olive oil

2 lemons, juiced

3 tomatoes, finely diced

salt and freshly ground black pepper, to taste

METHOD:

Place the burghul in a bowl and cover with the cold water, leaving it to soak until all of the water is absorbed, approximately 30 minutes. Cover the bowl with a cloth and set aside.

To prepare the parsley, shake off the excess moisture and remove any thick stalks. Wrap in a tea towel and place in the refrigerator to crisp and dry.

Place the burghul in a mixing bowl and add the spring onion, mixing well.

Chop the parsley and add it to the burghul with the mint and cucumber. In a separate jug or small bowl, beat the oil with the lemon juice. Add to the salad and toss well. Season to taste.

Gently mix the tomato through the salad. *Tabbouleh* is best when served chilled.

MUTTABAL

(roasted eggplant dip)

Like many Arab families, Samar's family loves to barbecue. On picnics especially, families gather around little charcoal barbecues, cooking kebabs and chicken wings. Whole eggplants are cooked over the coals, and then the women pound the eggplant into the freshest and most delicious *muttabal* dip (also known as *baba ghanoush*) to eat with hot flatbread. Samar serves her *muttabal* with a liberal sprinkling of ground sumac, which adds a lemony flavour to the dish.

Serves: 4 - 6 (as an appetiser)

INGREDIENTS:

1 eggplant (aubergine), about 375g (13oz)

60ml (2 fl oz or ¼ cup) lemon juice

65g (2 ¼ oz or ¼ cup) tahini

2 garlic cloves, crushed

1 teaspoon salt, or to taste

1 tablespoon olive oil

3 tablespoons finely chopped flat-leaf parsley, to garnish

optional garnish: dried ground sumac

METHOD:

Place the whole eggplant on the centre shelf of a preheated 200°C (400°F/Gas 6) oven, or charcoal barbecue, and cook until soft, turning 3 or 4 times.

Peel off the skin while the eggplant is still hot. Remove the stem.

Chop the flesh and pound to a purée using a mortar and pestle, or a blender or food processor. Blend in most of the lemon juice and gradually add the tahini. Add the crushed garlic. Beat well and adjust the flavour with more lemon juice and salt as desired. Mix in the oil.

Spread in a shallow serving dish, swirling the *muttabul* with the back of a spoon. Garnish with parsley and/or sumac and serve with flatbread, along with your favourite barbecue dishes.

UM OBEYDA

home: Homs, Syria
far from home since 2013

أم عبيدة

STORY KELLY FOWLER | **PHOTOGRAPHY** KATRINA FLETT GULBRANDSEN

"When I was due to deliver, the trouble was at its worst."

Um Obeyda's ginger-tinged hair is up in a messy ponytail when she answers the door. Her floral dress sticks a bit to her skin in the warmth of the day. The scent of herbs and broth thickens the afternoon air. She gives me a big hug and we kiss one another on the cheek. Waiting patiently for my sons to give her the traditional greeting, she bows to shake their hands. When they muddle the greeting, she flashes me a "whatever!" smile, her round cheeks flushed from work and cooking and children bustling around her.

Um Obeyda has a knack for sewing, having learned the skill after ending her studies in seventh grade in Syria. The beloved baby of ten children, she'd lost her father before entering her teens. She has sewn wedding dresses and suits through the years. When we worked together on a dress for me, she focused ruthlessly on details — the length of the sleeves as I moved, the type of fabric needed for the bodice — a pencil balanced between her teeth as she adjusted pins.

Married at twenty-two years old, her face colours slightly when she tells me her husband is referred to as a "gentleman" by friends. Ten years later, trouble started in Syria.

She explains, "I was thirty-two at the time and a month pregnant with my son (my fourth). The whole time we were there experiencing trouble, I was pregnant. When I was due to deliver, the trouble was at its worst. There was a government checkpoint right by our house, and rebels were on our roof and they were shooting at each other, some shooting up and some shooting down. We all hid in the bathroom for hours while the battle was going on, from sunset until morning."

When it came time for her son's delivery, Um Obeyda needed a cesarean because she could not risk going to the hospital at night during labour.

"Fifteen days after I had the baby we moved to Damascus. My husband wanted us to move before that, but I wanted to have the baby near my family. In Damascus we stayed with my sister-in-law, while my husband went to Jordan to look for a place for us to stay and for work."

The effort to get to Jordan and to safety took time and money and multiple attempts to cross the border. "After we were on the bus the officer saw us sitting there and said, 'Why are you sitting here? Go hide in the back. If a higher officer sees you, he won't let you go.' I was known there from all my previous attempts to cross!

"We were so thankful that this time they let us through. But when we arrived at the Jordanian side, their computers were down, and they searched everyone on the bus one by one. We left Damascus around 2 pm and didn't get into Jordan until 11 pm! It was a very hard trip, and the kids were young."

Nearly six years later, the family still waits for approval to emigrate. In the meantime, Um Obeyda's husband works as a barber at night when he can. In addition to sewing, Um Obeyda spends hours each week knitting to help support her family, in between managing the home and taking English lessons. She and her husband work together to keep their children studying and safely in school, their gaze fixed on the future of their children, on keeping their dreams alive. Their home remains full of life, children arriving sweaty from playing football, slinging their backpacks on the couch and shyly kissing me hello. They take my young sons under their wing as they play marbles or memory. Um Obeyda's daughter gently takes my youngest son on her lap, explaining a picture.

This afternoon, Um Obeyda and I make another batch of balm together, rekindling the warmth of a recent craft group balm-making session. She's grated the sticky block of beeswax into a curly amber pile. Today we melt the beeswax with oil made from locally harvested and pressed olives. We discuss the ratio of wax to oil and she concludes that more wax is needed as summer approaches. She sets the mixture over a shallow pan of boiling water and we set up little pots to hold the balm on her low-lying table. Her kitchen, immaculate and simple, boasts a small refrigerator, basic stove, and curtains shielding some pots, and pans. She pours the melted concoction into the pots and we wait while her son keeps checking the kitchen. "The balm is firming up!" he reports. We snack on cucumbers, talking about stretches for our sore shoulders and her dreams for her children.

Soon the balm, light buttery green and firm, is ready. We attach the lids to the pots, kissing our goodbyes, her eyes half-moons residing over her brave smile.

QATAYIF WA 'A'TAR

(stuffed pancakes with sugar syrup)

Every *Ramadan*, Muslim families prepare special sweets to enjoy once they break their daily fast. In Arab countries, one of these special sweets is *qatayif*. The pancakes are often sold pre-made from the local bakery, which does cut down the preparation time! The pancakes are then filled as tastes dictate - with cheese or nuts or even chocolate hazelnut spread! Um Obeyda prefers a creamy cheese filling.

Makes: 16 - 18

INGREDIENTS:

Pancake batter

2 teaspoons active dried yeast

1 teaspoon sugar

310ml (10 ½ fl oz or 1 ¼ cup) lukewarm water

225g (8 oz or 1 ½ cups) plain flour

pinch of salt

melted ghee or oil, for brushing

oil, for frying

Sugar syrup

500ml water

500g (1 lb 2 oz or 1 ½ cups) sugar

1 teaspoon lemon juice

1 - 2 tablespoons rosewater or orange blossom water

POSSIBLE FILLING VARIATIONS:

Nut filling

150g (5 oz or 1 ½ cups) finely chopped walnuts

55g (2 oz or ¼ cup) sugar

1 ½ teaspoons ground cinnamon

Cheese filling

250g (9 oz) ricotta cheese

Hazelnut spread and pistachio filling

1 jar of chocolate hazelnut spread

1 cup of chopped roasted pistachios

[omit the sugar syrup with this option]

METHOD:

Dissolve the yeast and sugar in the lukewarm water. Set aside until slightly foamy.

Sift the flour and salt into a mixing bowl and make a well in the centre. Pour the yeast mixture into the centre. Using a whisk, gradually stir the mixture until combined and smooth, removing all the lumps if possible.

Cover the bowl with a cloth and leave in a warm place for about an hour, or until the batter has risen and the surface is bubbly.

Meanwhile, make the sugar syrup. Bring water and the sugar to a boil in a heavy-based saucepan over medium heat, stirring occasionally. Add the lemon juice and simmer, without stirring, for 12 minutes, or until the syrup has thickened.

Add rosewater or orange blossom water to taste, then boil for a minute longer. When cool, the consistency should be similar to thin honey. Set aside.

Heat a non-stick frypan over a medium heat, and grease it with a paper towel dipped in oil, or canola spray.

Using a ladle, pour in about 1 ½ tablespoons of the batter in one lot and tilt the pan immediately so that the batter spreads into a circle about 10cm (4 inches) in diameter. If the batter is too thick, mix in a little extra water.

Cook the pancakes on one side only, for about 3 minutes, until the batter bubbles and is cooked through. They should look a bit like flattened crumpets. Stack the pancakes on a plate.

Prepare your chosen filling — either combine the nuts, sugar, and cinnamon in a bowl, or mash the cheese with a fork to soften it.

Place 2 generous teaspoons of filling in the centre of each pancake, on the uncooked side. Fold the pancake over and pinch the edges well together to seal.

For the hazelnut spread variation, apply the spread, sprinkle with pistachios, and omit the second frying step described below.

Heat a generous amount of oil in a frypan over a medium-high heat. Fry the stuffed pancakes three or four at a time for 2 or 3 minutes, turning to brown them evenly. Lift out with a slotted spoon and drain on paper towels.

Pile the pancakes onto a plate, pour over syrup to taste, and serve hot.

Bowls of fresh dates for the breaking of the Ramadan fast.

فلفل اسود
٤,٠٠٠ اوقية
بهارات
خليجية
٢,٥٠٠ اوقية
فلفل أبيض
٦,٠٠٠ اوقية

Spice market and perfumery, al-Balad, downtown Amman.

OLIVE OIL & BEESWAX BODY BALM murattib

with a Syrian handicraft group, Jordan

Olive oil can act as a cure-all for everything from shabby hair to jammed locks. Women swear by the power in its greenish hue to soften a person from the inside out. When asking friends how they keep their waist-length hair shiny and strong, they will confidently share instructions for a hair mask of olive oil, sure that it will change your hair — and your life. An older friend drinks a cup of olive oil a day, touting its role in his vitality as he ages. This balm serves as a simple way to make an olive oil remedy for all things skin and hair.

STORY KELLY FOWLER | **PHOTOGRAPHY** KATRINA FLETT GULBRANDSEN

MAKE IT:

olive oil and beeswax body balm – rose or orange blossom

Binding the olive oil with beeswax to form a balm makes the olive oil easy to contain and apply. The beeswax might be found in the local *atar* or in the *souk*, next to the black seed and cardamom pods. Bees are kept throughout Jordan as pollinators and producers of honey and wax. Our neighbour crafts his hives from old boxes and cardboard; he places them beneath olive and fig trees to optimise honey production and flavour.

YOU WILL NEED:

¼ cup shaved or chopped beeswax

1 cup olive oil

small saucepan

spoon

small funnel

small pots or jars with lids.
These can be found at craft stores, chemists or supermarkets, or alternatively use small recycled glass jars in different sizes. 12 small jars were required for this recipe.

rose or neroli (orange blossom) essential oils
These essences are used in a variety of skin care products, as well as to flavour sweets and drinks. Use 2.5 - 5ml (½ to 1 teaspoon) of essential oil per batch.

PROCESS:

As we make the balm, the women shave the blocks of wax with graters, releasing the sweet scent into the kitchen air. The olive oil and beeswax are carefully combined in a tin pot with a long straight handle (usually used to make Turkish coffee), and heated together over low heat. Stirring the warm concoction, the women banter by the stove. Soon the beeswax loses its shape to the olive oil. This is when an essential oil can be added, and the liquid is ready to pour into small pots.

In the hour we wait for the balm to firm, we gather around platters of *tabbouleh* and hand-made *fattayar*, and tell stories across the sitting room. Soon enough, we check the pots and the balm keeps its shape when prodded. We dip our fingers into a pot of balm and test different applications: cuticles, hair tips, elbows. Glossy heads nodding approval, ideas fly through the room about future variations and uses for the green-gold fix-all. A good evening turned to late night, bellies full and skin soft, we part ways.

SERENE

home: Beirut, Lebanon
far from home since 2003

سيرين

STORY & PHOTOGRAPHY KATRINA FLETT GULBRANDSEN

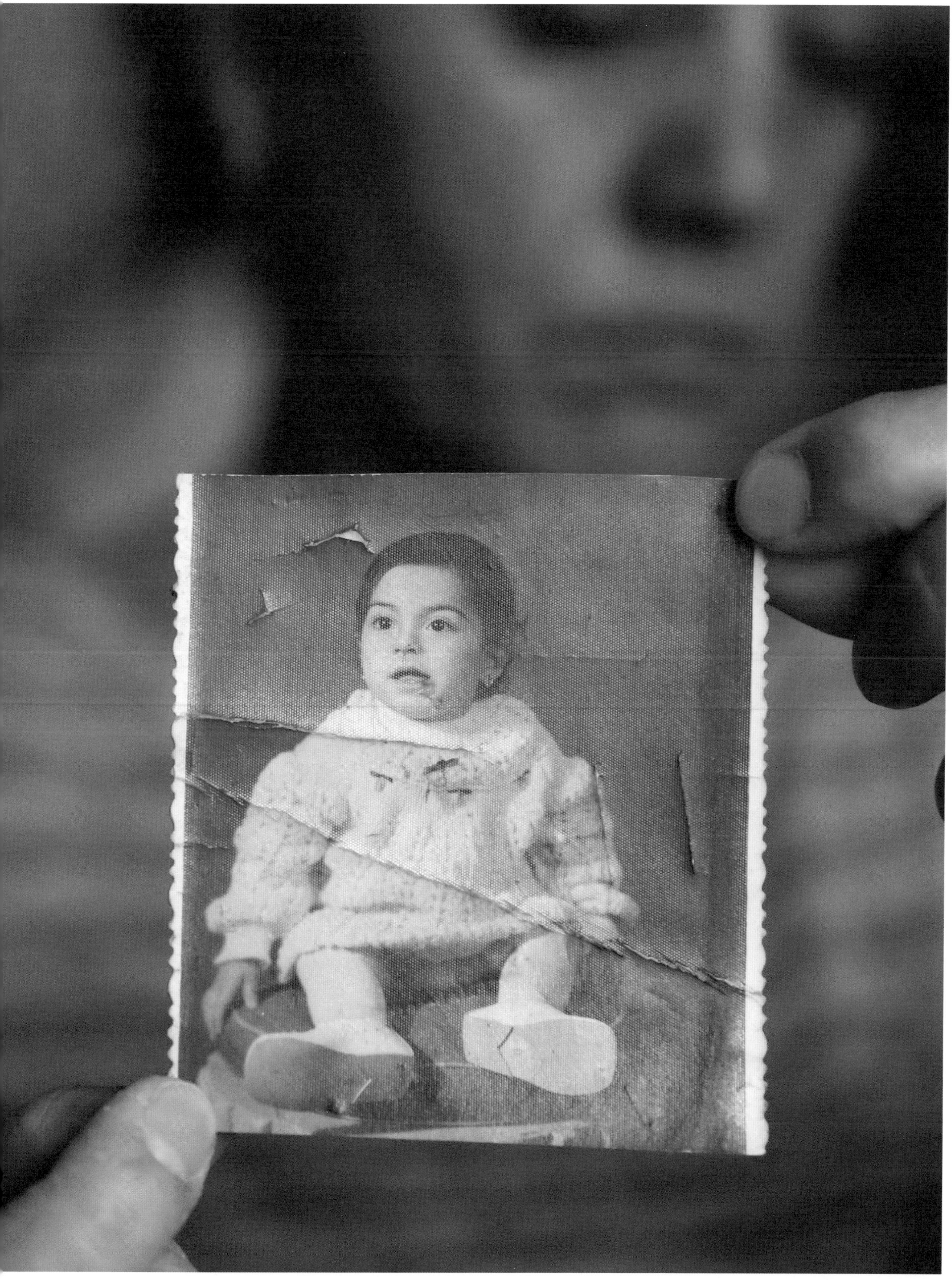

"Thunder isn't the promise of refreshing rain; it is fear, an explosion, a messenger with fatal news. My response is physical. I try to be rational, sensible, calm. I fail. I am always alert, always ready."

"Will you have tea?" Serene knows the answer to the question, and before I can answer, she stretches to reach the box of fragrant tea. "It comes from a special market in Sydney; you can't buy it here."

She deftly scoops the tea into a well-worn pot and sets it on the stove. Once boiled, she lets the tea rest. She draws our small children's attention to a colourful box of toys on the living room floor. The eldest children slam the back screen door on their way out to play soccer, and then... stillness, at least for a little while. She pours the warm amber liquid into two glasses, and we sit together, as we have become accustomed to doing.

"I take so many photos of the kids," she says. "My husband doesn't understand it at all. But I can still see my mother frantically searching amongst the garbage for just one photo, one tangible remnant of the life we lived before the war.

"I was four when we fled our house. I watched as my neighbours and once-friends — now enemies — unapologetically carried off all my family's possessions. But furniture and things mean nothing. My mother wanted to save our memories.

"My mother held it to her chest, the torn photo of me, her child, as if to defy anyone to take it from her again; her treasure found amongst the refuse, now disentombed. I still have this photo, the only one salvaged on that vivid and dehumanising day. We never went back to our home, or our neighbourhood...

"Five of my uncles were killed — no, four, and one cousin. It was a long time ago now. It is still hard to talk about... I remember my aunties crying; how do you say goodbye without a body to grieve over? Alone, with small mouths to feed, rumours of rape and kidnapping rampant...

"And my grandfather... I loved my grandfather; he fed me breakfast every morning. One day he didn't come home from the mosque. They found his body two weeks later."

Serene glances outside to check the children. Another memory comes to her.

"I remember her backpack, all yellow and silver. It was special — sent from Germany just for her. It sat by the wall in our house, long after she died. She was eight years old, my sister's best friend. She died on a hospital bed, embedded with shrapnel from the bomb that erupted in our front yard. I try to forget the dust, the glass, and the blood... Eight of my friends died that day...

"Thunder isn't the promise of refreshing rain; it is fear, an explosion, a messenger with fatal news. My response is physical. I try to be rational, sensible, calm. I fail. I am always alert, always ready."

"That's enough now... Would you like another tea?"

Serene refills my glass. "Cherish your family!" she says, "Don't be afraid of those who are different; we must all work together."

Serene could be bitter, but she is not. A little broken, she is brave and honest enough to admit it.

The screen door slams again, our eldest children barge into the living room. Our tea time is over for today.

Serene serves as an Arabic/English interpreter with the healthcare service in an Australian town that recently received more than three hundred Syrians for resettlement. She also volunteers at a centre for refugee women, where she provides psycho-social support and assists with recreational programs. Serene's experiences of civil war in Lebanon and as an immigrant in Australia motivate her compassionate work with the newly arrived.

MASHRUUBAAT

(drinks)

One of Serene's favourite drinks is *shay ma na'na*, a sweetened blend of mint and Ceylon tea, included in the following recipes. In Arab homes, special occasions will usually open with something cold and refreshing, followed by tea. Strong, thick coffee is often served as a closure to evenings shared with friends and family.

SHAY MA NA'NA

(Arabic mint tea)

Serves: 4

INGREDIENTS:

1L (34 fl oz or 4 cups) water

1 ½ tablespoons high quality Ceylon loose leaf tea

8 sprigs fresh mint

2 ½ tablespoons sugar (or to taste)

METHOD:

Boil the water in a kettle and let it sit for about 1 minute to cool slightly. Place the tea and four sprigs of mint into a teapot or saucepan. Add the water and steep for 2 - 5 minutes. Place the remaining sprigs in 4 clear tea glasses and pour the tea, adding sugar to taste.

KARKADE

(hibiscus and cinnamon herbal tea)

Serves: 4

INGREDIENTS:

1L (34 fl oz or 4 cups) water

3 tablespoons dried hibiscus flowers

1 medium cinnamon stick

2 ½ tablespoons sugar (or to taste)

METHOD:

Place water, hibiscus flowers, and cinnamon stick in a medium saucepan and bring to a boil. Reduce heat and simmer gently for 5 minutes. Pour into clear tea glasses and add sugar as desired. Alternatively, the sugar may be added to the saucepan and stirred thoroughly until dissolved. This tea can also be cooled and refrigerated for a refreshing summer drink!

ASEER AL LEYMON MA NA'NA

(lemon and mint juice)

Serves: 4

INGREDIENTS:

3 - 4 lemons, cut in half and juiced

1L (34 fl oz or 4 cups) chilled water

115g (3 ¾ oz or ½ cup) caster sugar

1 cup mint leaves, washed

1 teaspoon orange blossom water (optional)

METHOD:

Place the lemon juice, chilled water, washed mint leaves, sugar, and orange blossom water into a blender. Blend until the mint is very finely chopped, but still visible.

Note: Adjust the lemon, mint, and sugar quantities to your taste. In the Middle East the drink is made very sweet, sweeter than the above recipe! If you're going for a truly authentic taste, use up to a cup of sugar.

Variation: For an icy version of this drink, mix the water and lemon juice, pour into ice-cube trays and freeze. Blend the ice cubes with the sugar and mint as above, and serve with a straw and spoon.

QAHWEH

(Turkish coffee)

Serves: 4

INGREDIENTS:

500ml (17 fl oz or 2 cups) water

20g (¾ oz or ¼ cup) Turkish coffee (very finely ground dark roast coffee)

2 - 4 teaspoons sugar, according to your preference

6 cardamom pods (optional)

METHOD:

Turkish coffee is the grind of choice for most people in the Middle East. There are many different schools of practice when preparing Turkish coffee. We include the method most commonly used by our hosts, who usually use a long-handled *rakwah* coffee pot and demitasse cups for serving.

Heat the water in a small saucepan or *rakwah*. Add the desired amount of sugar and stir to dissolve. Add the coffee and cardamom, if using, and stir over medium-low heat. When the coffee rises in the pot, remove the pot from the heat, and spoon some froth into each cup. Repeat once or twice more, spooning the froth out each time, then pour the coffee into the cups.

SHAY BIL MIRAMYA MA NA'NA

(Bedouin sage & mint tea)

Savoured by Bedouins and their guests throughout the Middle East, this sweet, aromatic tea blends sage and mint — found around the springs in the desert — with black Ceylon tea and copious amounts of sugar. This tea will cool you on a hot, dry day as you sit in the shade of a black woven tent; it will warm you on a cold and clear desert evening as you gather around a smoky fire beneath the stars.

Here we provide instructions for drying, blending, and brewing your own sage and mint tea. Depending on individual taste, the quantities can be adjusted as desired.

Makes approximately 1 ½ cups of loose leaf tea blend

YOU WILL NEED:

1 bunch of fresh sage
(to make approximately ½ cup chopped dried sage)

1 bunch of fresh mint
(to make approximately ½ cup chopped dried mint)

½ cup large-leaf Ceylon tea
(can be bought in an Asian food store)

paper bags (2 - 4)

string

a sharp knife

AIR DRYING YOUR FRESH HERBS:

Bundle 5 - 10 stalks of each herb separately and tie each with string (remember if the bunch is big, it will take longer for the herbs to dry).

Place each bunch upside down into a paper bag, with a few holes cut in the bottom of the bag for ventilation.

Take the top of the bag and close it around the herb stems and tie with more string.

Hang the herbs upside down in a warm, dry, and well -ventilated room for 1 - 2 weeks. When completely dry, they should crumble easily.

If you do not wish to use the dried herbs immediately, store them in an airtight container out of direct sunlight.

BLENDING YOUR HERBS & TEA:

Using a sharp knife, chop the large-leaf tea, dried mint, and sage separately, into approximately 5mm pieces.

Take half a cup of each chopped ingredient and pour into a bowl, mix well, and store in an airtight container.

To create a unique gift, try placing the tea into small tea tins and labelling with *shay* — tea, in Arabic calligraphy: شاي (see calligraphy instructions on pages 148 - 149).

BREWING:

Place 1 - 2 teaspoons of tea blend per cup of boiling water in a pot or tea glass and let it steep for 3 - 5 minutes. Add sugar to taste — traditionally this drink is served very sweet!

MARUWA

home: Homs, Syria
far from home since 2013

مروى

STORY TARYN LAMMI | **PHOTOGRAPHY** KATRINA FLETT GULBRANDSEN

بسم الله الرحمن الرحيم
قل هو الله احد
الله الصمد
لم يلد ولم يولد
ولم يكن له
كفوا احد
صدق الله العظيم

"If you love somebody, then you do whatever they say. We love God, and so because He has told us to wear the hijab, we're going to wear it."

There was a knock at my door. I opened it to see my language tutor, Maruwa — sixteen years old and covered from head to toe in loose, black polyester, only her smiling eyes visible. She had arrived to give me an Arabic lesson.

"Ahlan wa Sahlan. Itfaddali!"

"Shukran habibti! Keefik?"

We exchanged kisses. With the door to the outside world shut, she removed her *niqab*, leaving only her *hijab* covering her hair, and we began our lesson.

Most days we would start out seriously, but in no time we would relax and start joking around. An online translation program was our best friend during these times. Hand gestures and charades also helped our communication, and provided lots of laughs. We are only a few years apart in age. I was in Jordan volunteering with a small organisation assisting refugees, before starting my university studies.

Maruwa's education has been interrupted. One day she would like to become a doctor; however her access to education is limited. Her family is doing everything in its power to help her continue learning, but higher education and employment opportunities are beyond reach for most Syrian refugees in Jordan.

After claiming asylum in Jordan, Maruwa's family applied for the UNHCR resettlement program. The family underwent a rigorous screening process and attended many detailed interviews. After a lengthy wait, they were told that France and Austria were considering their resettlement applications. Soon after, they received the news that France would accept them.

"We were all excited," Maruwa said, and they continued with the process. When they were required to be photographed, they learned that the girls would not be allowed to keep their *hijabs* on. Furthermore, in France, Maruwa would not be permitted to wear a headscarf in school. "Knowing these two things," Amal, Maruwa's mother said, "we refused." While their situation in Jordan is untenable in the long term, they were not willing to compromise their conviction to gain entry to France.

"If you love somebody," Maruwa said, "then you do whatever they say. We love God, and so because He has told us to wear the *hijab*, we're going to wear it."

And so they continue to wait, dedicated to their faith, and hoping for a path forward for Maruwa's dream of a career in medicine. For the time being, Maruwa attends after-hours lessons at the local school. She spends the rest of her time with her books, preparing for an uncertain future.

After our two hours of Arabic, we wondered where the time went! As my mind swam with beautiful new Arabic words and phrases, Maruwa prepared to leave. Quickly and expertly she replaced her *niqab*. Looking forward to our next lesson, I called out the door: *"Bashoufik badayn!"*

She called back, *"Inshallah!"*

الحمد لله رب العالمين

SFIHA

(flatbread with toppings)

One day Maruwa's father and his friend overheard the local butcher complaining that he needed someone to make *sfiha* for his shop. His friend looked at him and said "Can you make *sfiha*?" He replied, "Yes, of course!" And so began a family business. Maruwa's mother mixes and kneads the dough in an enormous tub on her kitchen floor before it is scurried away by Maruwa to her father and younger brothers outside in the small courtyard. Here they are busy cutting, rolling, topping, and baking the *sfiha* in their outdoor oven. Flour falls everywhere. The scent of the baking dough fills the air. Later in the day, the brothers carry trays of this tasty and much-loved snack to the butcher.

Makes about 30

INGREDIENTS:

BREAD DOUGH

450g (1 lb or 3 cups) plain flour, plus extra for kneading

10g (2 teaspoons) active dried yeast

1 ½ teaspoons salt

1 teaspoon sugar

1 tablespoon oil

250ml (8 fl oz or 1 cup) warm water

METHOD:

Place the flour into a large mixing bowl and set aside in a warm place. Dissolve the yeast in the warm water, stir in the salt and sugar, and leave for 5 minutes or until slightly foamy. The yeast will not foam if the water is too hot or too cold.

Pour the yeast liquid into the centre of the flour and stir, adding the oil gradually. Beat until smooth, either by hand for 10 minutes, or with an electric mixer using a dough hook for 5 minutes.

Sprinkle some of the reserved flour onto a surface; knead the dough for 10 minutes or until it is smooth and even in texture. Place the dough in an oiled bowl, then turn it over to coat the top with oil. Cover and leave to rise at room temperature until it has at least doubled in size.

Cut the dough into several long strips and roll out like long thin sausages (approximately 3cm or 1 inch in diameter). Using a sharp knife, cut the rolls of dough into 2cm or ¾-inch discs. On a well-floured surface, roll out the discs until paper thin. Stack the discs using baking paper or lots of flour to prevent sticking.

Recipe continued on next page

INGREDIENTS:

OPTION 1 - vegetable & meat topping

500g (1 lb 2 oz) minced beef or lamb

1 large onion, finely diced

2 cloves of garlic, finely diced

1 red capsicum (bell pepper), finely diced

1 green capsicum, finely diced

½ teaspoon (dried) sumac, (x 3 if using fresh sumac)

½ cup of parsley leaves, chopped

salt and pepper, to season

125g (4 oz or 1 cup) chopped, peeled tomatoes

2 tablespoons of pomegranate molasses*

OPTION 2 - meat topping

500g (1 lb 2 oz) minced beef or lamb

2 large onions, finely diced

180ml (6 fl oz or ¾ cup) tahini

250ml (8 fl oz or 1 cup) pomegranate molasses*

salt and pepper, to season

To finish

oil, for brushing

pomegranate seeds, lemon wedges, yoghurt, to serve

METHOD:

Preheat the oven to 200°C (400°F/Gas 6).

To make the vegetable & meat topping, heat the oil in a frypan, add the meat, and stir over medium-high heat until the meat is browned and crumbly. Add the onion and gently fry until the onion has softened. Add the capsicum, garlic, and sumac and season well. Fry for 1 minute longer, then stir in the parsley and tomatoes. Cover and cook over low heat for 10 minutes, or until the tomato softens.

Stir in the pomegranate molasses. Remove from the heat and leave to cool. The mixture should be moist, but not liquid.

Alternatively, to make the meat topping, heat the oil in a frypan, add the meat, and stir over medium-high heat until the meat is browned and crumbly. Add the onion and gently fry until the onion has softened. Add the tahini and pomegranate molasses and heat for 1 minute. Season to taste.

Take a round of dough and spread 3 tablespoons of your chosen filling on the top, not quite to the edge. Place the *sfiha* close together on oiled baking trays. Brush the meat and dough edge lightly with oil.

Bake the *sfiha* on a tray lined with baking paper for 12 - 15 minutes. Serve hot or warm, sprinkled with a few fresh pomegranate seeds, if available. *Sfiha* are lovely with a side of lemon wedges and yoghurt.

*You may substitute the pomegranate molasses with tomato paste and sugar. Use 1 teaspoon of sugar for each tablespoon of tomato paste.

FATTAYAR

(cheese boats)

Maruwa's family also bakes batch after batch of *fattayar* in their outside oven. These are a breakfast favourite — a soft doughy vessel for a delectable melted cheese filling seasoned with parsley and onion seeds.

Makes: 15

INGREDIENTS:

375g (13 oz or 2 ½ cups) plain flour

1 tablespoon active dried yeast

1 tablespoon sugar

½ teaspoon salt

190ml (6 fl oz or ¾ cup) milk, lukewarm

80ml (3 fl oz or ⅓ cup) olive oil, plus extra for brushing

125g (4 ½ oz or ½ cup) feta cheese

125g (4 ½ oz or ½ cup) mozzarella cheese, grated

4 tablespoons parsley, finely chopped

2 teaspoons onion seeds

1 egg, beaten

METHOD:

Preheat the oven to 200°C (400°F/Gas 6).

Combine yeast, sugar, salt, and milk in a large jug and set aside for 5 minutes or until foamy.

Place the flour in a large bowl, and add the milk mixture. Stir with a flat knife until combined. Alternatively, process in a food processor. Add the olive oil and knead for 3 - 4 minutes until smooth and silky. Place in an oiled bowl, cover and allow to rise for 10 minutes or so.

Soak the feta in cold water for 10 minutes, changing the water twice.

Crumble the feta in a bowl and add the mozzarella cheese, egg, onion seeds, and parsley. Toss to combine well.

Roll the dough out to 1cm (½-inch) thickness and cut into rounds with a cup or biscuit cutter. Alternatively, roll the dough into balls the size of small eggs. Stretch your circles or roll out the balls into ovals. Place a tablespoon of the cheese mixture in the middle.

Fold both edges over to create a canoe-like shape as shown in the pictures. Place the *fattayar* close together on oiled baking trays. Brush lightly with oil.

Bake for about 15 - 20 minutes. Serve hot.

Girls on their walk to school, Mafraq, Jordan.

SHAHINEZ

home: Mosul, Iraq
far from home since 2014

شهناز

STORY SALLY BATHGATE | **PHOTOGRAPHY** SOPHIE TIMOTHY

"We are not allowed to hate. I do not hate because Jesus loves."

We gather outside our local Jordanian church after the service, my family chatting with Shahinez and her sons and daughter. Shahinez invites us to join them for lunch at home. There has been progress on their application to resettle in Australia, and Shahinez wants to discuss it with us.

We cross the narrow road to their small flat, provided to them by the church after they arrived from Iraq. While her daughter finishes the meal preparations in the kitchen, Shahinez shares some of her stories.

Her own recent eviction from her home in Mosul echoes the history of her grandparents during the Armenian genocide. She tells me about her grandmother and other relatives who were orphaned, displaced, oppressed, and mistreated in their Ottoman homeland. I am struck by the story of her grandfather, who as a young man had come to live in Mosul in search of religious freedom.

"When my grandfather was seven years old, he and his two young cousins escaped from Turkey. This was during the Armenian genocide in 1915 - 1917. They were the only ones from their whole tribe to survive. After their escape, they came to live on the border between Turkey and Iraq and were raised by a Kurdish Muslim family. They were Christians; and as they grew, they realised their Christian beliefs were in conflict with the beliefs of their foster family. They eventually moved to Iraq so they could continue living freely as Christians. My grandfather finally settled in Mosul, as did many other Christians.

"Mosul is a beautiful city located on the Tigris River. My home was very close to the river, near a bridge that we walked across every day. The city was full of green nature, with a very nice climate. There were many churches all around Mosul.

"Before the fall of Iraq State [2003], we were not oppressed for being Christians. But after it fell, we became increasingly threatened. In 2004, the Christians became targets of different parties in Mosul. They began to punish us for being Christians; identifying us by our names.

"The security of the city became progressively more unstable, and we feared kidnapping at every moment. Then on June 4th, 2014, Mosul came under siege and was overtaken by different militias. We escaped from the city and fled to a Christian village called Dahuk. We hoped that the situation would get better — but it got worse. Within months, ISIS [Islamic State in Iraq and Syria] declared control over the region. They began to persecute the Christians

noomi — dried limes

and take their homes. Christian houses were marked with the symbol 'ن' [the first character of a word for Christian in Arabic, used pejoratively]. They issued rules concerning Christians. They stopped the salaries of Christian employees and stopped their food supply cards. In the middle of July, they announced a time limit to choose between being killed, becoming Muslims, or leaving.

"So other Christians began to leave. Those that did not leave by the end of the time limit, ISIS began to harm."

Echoing stories of the Armenian genocide one hundred years ago, Shahinez speaks of the violence suffered by her fellow Christians at the hands of ISIS.

Listening to Shahinez speak, I wonder at her lack of bitterness, and bluntly ask in my broken Arabic, "With all that has happened to you as Christians, do you hate the Muslims who have done these terrible things?"

She tells me one story that has particularly challenged her towards forgiveness.

"There was a mother of two girls. ISIS entered her house while one of the girls was taking a shower. The mother begged the men to give her some time, until her daughter had finished her shower. They refused and burnt the house while the girl was still in the bathroom. The daughter died after two or three days in the hospital, and her last words were, 'I forgive them like Jesus'."

Shahinez looks me in the eye as we consider this martyred girl's impulse to forgive.

Shahinez's eyes are careworn — she is so far from home, but she finds consolation in her faith and in the possibility it offers of forgiveness and reconciliation.

"We grieve for our country, homes, places of birth. We have such beautiful memories of our country. We did not want to leave. We wanted to live in brotherhood, but we were forced to leave Iraq. I pray daily for Iraq and the Middle East. I pray for ISIS. We forgive them and pray for them to know Jesus, the living God, who is the way and life.

"All people are God's creatures; we are all brothers. We are not allowed to hate. I do not hate because Jesus loves."

An Easter service in a Greek Orthodox church, Amman, Jordan.

TASHREEB

(stewed lamb shanks)

This delicious stew contains a favourite ingredient in Middle Eastern cooking, *noomi* (dried lime), which gives this dish a distinctive citrus taste. Adding to the depth of flavour, many cooks infuse their *tashreeb* with a whole bulb of garlic. If you prefer to omit the garlic, you're in good company. Leave it out in solidarity with Shahinez!

Serves: 6

INGREDIENTS:

6 lamb shanks

250g (1 lb 2 oz or 1 cup) dried chickpeas, soaked overnight, then drained*

2 *noomi* (dried limes) pierced twice, or thinly peeled zest of ½ a lemon

1 garlic bulb, left whole, but washed and peeled of outer layer

60ml (2 fl oz or ¼ cup) oil

1 large onion, finely chopped

500g (1 lb 2 oz or 3 cups) tomatoes, peeled and chopped

60g (2 oz or ¼ cup) tomato paste (concentrated purée)

1 teaspoon *baharat* spice blend, optional (recipe p. 78)

3 - 4 bay leaves

salt and freshly ground black pepper, to season

2 large flatbreads (recipe p. 142)

METHOD:

Place the lamb shanks and chickpeas in a large saucepan and cover with cold water. Add the dried limes or lemon rind and the whole garlic bulb. Bring to a boil and simmer slowly, skimming the fat as required.

Meanwhile, heat the oil in a frypan and gently fry the onion for 2 - 5 minutes. Add the tomatoes, tomato paste, *baharat*, and bay leaves.

When the lamb is well-skimmed and simmering, add the tomato mixture and season with salt and pepper. Cover and simmer gently for 2 - 2 ½ hours, or until the lamb is tender.

Remove the limes or rind, bay leaves, and the garlic bulb and discard. Remove the lamb from the pan. Strip the meat from the bones and shred or cut into pieces, then return the meat to the pan.

Cut the bread into pieces and place at the bottom of each bowl or deep plate. Ladle the stew on top of the bread and serve.

*You may use a can of chickpeas instead, adding them 15 minutes before the end of the cooking time.

SUNIYET BATATA BIL LAHEM

(lamb and mashed potato bake)

This sultana-rich recipe, much loved in Mosul, is one of Shahinez's favourite comfort foods. It's a bit like a Middle Eastern twist on shepherd's pie.

Serves: 6

INGREDIENTS:

MASHED POTATOES:

1kg (2 lb 3 oz) potatoes, whole and unpeeled

1 tablespoon butter

2 tablespoons milk

½ teaspoon cumin

salt, to taste

FILLING:

500g (1 lb 2 oz) minced beef or lamb

1 tablespoon olive oil

1 onion, finely chopped

90g (3 oz or 1 cup) mushrooms, sliced

200g (7 oz or ¾ cup) sultanas (raisins)

½ teaspoon black pepper

¼ teaspoon chilli

1 teaspoon *baharat**

salt, to taste

TOPPING:

250g (9 oz or 1 cup) cheddar or mozzarella, grated

METHOD:

Preheat the oven to 180°C (350°F/Gas 4). Grease a medium-sized oven dish or roasting pan with oil.

Boil the whole potatoes in a large pot of salted water until the potatoes are cooked and the skin has loosened. Drain the potatoes and rinse with cool water. Peel off and discard the skins. Process the potatoes in a food processor or mash well by hand. Add the butter, milk, and cumin and mix well.

Meanwhile, heat the oil in a frypan and gently fry the lamb and onion for 5 minutes, then add the mushrooms, sultanas, and spices. Cook for a further 5 minutes or until cooked through, and season to taste.

Place half the mashed potato in the roasting pan and flatten to the edges with the back of a spoon. Cover the potato with the minced lamb mixture, and then layer on the other half of the potato. Sprinkle the cheese over the top layer of potato.

Bake in the oven for 15 minutes, and serve with your favourite Middle Eastern salad.

**Baharat* is a Middle Eastern blend of spices available in some specialty stores or Middle Eastern grocers. Like Indian *masala*, every household's *baharat* blend is slightly different. You could make your own *baharat* by mixing 4 parts black pepper, 4 parts cumin, 3 parts coriander seeds, 3 parts cinnamon, 3 parts cloves, 1 part cardamom, 3 parts nutmeg, and 6 parts paprika. For best results, grind whole freshly toasted spices. You can adjust the blend to your own taste.

Church and neighbouring mosque, Jerash, Jordan.

Women pray in a Greek Orthodox Church, Jordan.

PALM WEAVING tajdeel al nakhil

with Halah

Halah grips the palm frond between her knees and uses her fingernail to slice up a palm leaf, splitting it in two. She repeats the process until a large section of the frond is shredded into streamer-like strips.

"There," she says, "We are ready! My mother loved to learn, and to teach our old traditions to others. Now I pass these crafts on to my children."

I have come to Halah's home to learn the craft of *sha'neeneh* palm weaving. After sharing a traditional *mansaf* for lunch, we move to the porch, where Halah serves tea and invites me to sit beside her. Her son brings us a bundle of palm fronds from the garden. As Halah weaves, I observe each step, attempting to duplicate her moves.

Halah is originally from a village called Al Hoson in Jordan. She has been weaving palm fronds to celebrate the Greek Orthodox *sha'neeneh* or Palm Sunday service, for as long as she can remember.

The weaving of palm fronds to celebrate Palm Sunday is an ancient art, practiced by Christians throughout the Middle East. Palm Sunday commemorates Jesus's triumphant entry into Jerusalem just prior to his crucifixion; it is celebrated on the last Sunday before Easter.

According to the Gospels, many people in Jerusalem took their cloaks and branches, and laid them down on the road before Jesus as he rode into the city on a young colt. Many Middle Eastern churches re-enact this joyous and colourful event with a procession around the church, where children wave their homemade *sha'neeneh*; calling out, "Hosanna in the highest!" as in the Biblical account.

I follow Halah as she folds the tail ends into her weaving and trims them. My *sha'neeneh* is nearly finished, and Halah expresses joy over my work. She fills her *sha'neeneh* with geranium, honeysuckle, and rosemary, threading the stems through the weaving. She holds up our woven fronds with delight and the children come around to see them.

STORY & PHOTOGRAPHY KATRINA FLETT GULBRANDSEN

MAKE IT:

palm weaving

Some palm weavings are simple to create, while others are extremely complicated. The instructions and pictures included here will enable you to weave your own traditional *sha'neeneh* from a palm frond. These look beautiful in a vase, and when dry, they curl and lighten, making an interesting sculptural form.

YOU WILL NEED:

One palm frond — Look for a frond from a pinnate palm (which resembles a feather). The frond will have two rows of leaves on each side of the stem. See picture.

A sharp knife or scissors

palm weaving continued on next page

PROCESS:

1. Take approximately a ½ meter section from the tip end of a palm frond. Using a knife, remove the lower leaves, so you have a handle-sized stem to hold or to place in a vase.
2. Sit and place the handle-like stem firmly between your knees.
3. Using your thumb nail, pierce the bottom right leaf at the base through the middle. Gently slide your nail through the leaf to the very tip, splitting it into 2 pieces. Repeat this with the next 2 leaves and then do the same on the left side. Now you will have 12 palm ribbons to use as you weave.
4. Pull down the first bottom ribbon on each side of the stem. Twist the left ribbon counter-clockwise, twist the right ribbon clockwise, then turn both up and cross them in front of the stem, right over left.
5. Holding the crossing point firmly, take the second right ribbon and weave it under the left ribbon. Adjust your grip to hold the growing weave pattern.
6. Take the second ribbon from the left, then weave it over and under the already-woven ribbons.
7. Take the third ribbon from the right and weave it over/under.
8. Take the third ribbon from the left and weave it under/over/under.
9. Take the fourth ribbon from the right and weave it under/over/under.
10. Continue this way until all 12 ribbons are woven together to form a cone-like shape.
11. Starting from the top-most point, fold the end of each ribbon over the edge of the cone and tuck it back in on itself, weaving it under a ribbon segment to secure it. Alternatively, you can leave some strands out to curl. Use scissors or a knife to trim the ends as desired.

The *sha'neeneh* can be filled or threaded through with fresh flowers, placed in a vase, or allowed to dry.

To add additional cones to the stem (as pictured on right), move up the stem, and begin again from step 3.

MARYAM

home: Iran

far from home since birth, 1992

مریم

STORY & PHOTOGRAPHY KATRINA FLETT GULBRANDSEN

"I dream of a place where I can grow; a place where I am not limited by my nationality."

I'm at an all-women's swimming pool in Amman, Jordan. Women and children crowd together in the shallow end, shoulder to shoulder, laughing and screaming. I slide into the empty deep end reluctantly. The water is cloudy — I definitely can't see the tiles on the bottom. As I breaststroke up the pool, trying to keep my head above whatever might be in the water, I wonder if my health will suffer from this mid-summer indulgence. I first see her sitting by the edge; she is studying me intensely with huge brown eyes, watching every cautious stroke. We make eye contact. She says, "Where are you from?"

Two years later we sit opposite each other, good friends, on a balcony in a busy café, in down-town Amman. "Do you remember the first time I met you?" she says. Her thickly lined eyes are still large and shining, radiating intelligence and humour. Her long hair hangs around her shoulders — although a Muslim, she chooses not to wear a head covering, believing that God is more concerned with what's *inside* her head.

She leans back and draws in her breath, sucking in the sweet, apple-scented smoke from her *argilah*. The water gurgles soothingly and she blows out a billow of smoke. She smiles and says, "I thought to myself, *She can swim! I must get to know her.*"

Maryam is beautiful. She is positive, kind, hard-working, and ambitious. But every now and then — when she becomes weary and disappointed, she is overtaken by the long shadow that has stalked her since birth: being a foreigner in her home country.

"The thing is," she says, "my father is Iranian and my mother is Jordanian. I, like my father, am Iranian. I have an Iranian passport, but cannot live in Iran. I was born in Jordan. I've lived in Jordan all my life, but I am not legally a Jordanian nor am I considered one. This is my reality and the reality for many other people like me. Where do we belong? We are treated as foreigners in the country of our birth, the only country that many of us know. Is this fair and right?"

Jordanian law does not currently allow Jordanian mothers to confer citizenship on their children; only fathers have this right. Lack of citizenship has serious implications for Maryam, reducing her access to health care, education and employment. It creates lifelong logistical and financial issues, but also has serious social and psychological consequences. Maryam feels Jordanian, but she is constantly reminded by the system, and those around her, that she is not. "I am treated like a terrorist," she says, with a tint of dark humour. "I just tell them to back off and get out of my face!"

Against financial and social hardships, Maryam fought for and attained a Bachelor of Business Administration in 2014, coming first in her class. She was the first member of her family to study at university. She now studies Farsi and English in her limited spare time, works long hours at a low-paying job for which she is overqualified, and helps to support her family. She refuses to be intimidated by stereotypes, discrimination, and a system that works against her. She puts on a strong face, works hard, and sometimes allows herself to dream of further study and working abroad.

One long puff on the *argilah* sends the last cloud of dangerously delicious apple smoke to envelop us both – she has become a true friend during my time in Jordan, and I wish I could do something tangible to assist her in her climb up over the injustice. When I ask her what she hopes for most of all, she says, "I dream of a place where I can grow; a place where I am not limited by my nationality." We hug, and she walks out the canary yellow café door with confident steps that mask her vulnerability.

Note: Jordan is currently considering citizenship law reform and the rights of children born to Jordanian women.

Maryam's graduation photo sits among her father's treasures in their living room.

SAHLAB

(hot milk and blossom drink)

When wandering the old streets of Amman on cool evenings, Maryam and her friends often stop to buy paper cups filled with steaming, thick and sweet *sahlab*. The milky treat often comes garnished with coconut, cinnamon, and almonds, although Maryam prefers hers ungarnished — the rose and orange blossom flavours are delicious on their own.

Serves: 4

INGREDIENTS:

60g (2 oz or ½ cup) cornflour (cornstarch)

½ cup boiling water

1L (34 fl oz or 4 cups) milk

4 tablespoons sugar (or to taste)

1 tablespoon rose water

1 tablespoon orange blossom water

For garnish (optional):

1 tablespoon crushed almonds

1 teaspoon cinnamon

1 tablespoon coconut

METHOD:

In a heat-proof bowl or mug, place the cornflour (cornstarch) and add boiling water, stirring quickly until the flour has dissolved.

In a heavy-based saucepan, place milk, sugar, rose water, and orange blossom water. Stir, over low heat, until warm. Add the cornflour mixture and stir constantly until the liquid has thickened. Pour into mugs and top with cinnamon, crushed almonds, and coconut as desired. You will need a spoon!

A café popular with students in al-Balad, downtown Amman.

MJEDERRA

(lentils and rice with crispy onion)

Mjederra is a dish of many parts, and many cooking pots. You may need as many as five saucepans and frypans! However, you needn't cook everything at the same time — you can prepare the lentils, rice, macaroni, and sauce ahead of meal time as it suits your daily routine. Choose the topping of your choice — Maryam opts for the cucumber salad rather than the tomato purée, which is generally preferred in Egyptian versions of this dish *(koushari)*.

Serves: 6

INGREDIENTS:

185g (6 ½ oz or 1 cup) green lentils, rinsed well

2 teaspoons salt

220g (8 oz or 1 cup) short-grain white rice

2 tablespoons olive oil

155g (5 oz or 1 cup) macaroni

½ teaspoon cumin

½ teaspoon turmeric

For garnish:

2 onions, halved and very thinly sliced

oil, for frying

TO SERVE:

OPTION 1 - cucumber salad

250ml (8 ½ fl oz or 1 cup) natural yoghurt

1 large Lebanese cucumber, finely chopped

1 garlic clove, crushed

1 handful fresh mint leaves, roughly chopped

salt and freshly ground black pepper

OPTION 2 - tomato purée

2 tablespoons olive oil

1 small onion, finely diced

2 garlic cloves, crushed

250ml (8 ½ fl oz or 1 cup) tomato purée or passata

1 teaspoon *baharat* spice blend*

salt and freshly ground black pepper

METHOD:

Place the washed lentils in a saucepan with 750ml (25 fl oz or 3 cups) water and 1 teaspoon of the salt. Bring to a boil, then reduce the heat and simmer, uncovered, for one hour or until the lentils are tender. Drain and set aside.

While the lentils are simmering, prepare the rice. Heat the olive oil in a saucepan over moderate heat. Add the rice and the other teaspoon of the salt and fry gently for 2 minutes. Add 500ml (17 fl oz or 2 cups) of water, stir well, and bring to a boil. Once boiling, reduce the heat to low and simmer, covered, for 15 minutes. Remove from the heat.

Meanwhile, prepare the macaroni in a separate saucepan following the packet instructions.

Prepare the onion garnish by heating sufficient oil in a saucepan, adding the onions, and deep-frying until brown and crispy. Remove from the oil and drain on paper towel. Leave to cool.

Place the macaroni in a large dish and coat with a little extra olive oil. Add the rice and lentils and mix through. Sprinkle with the cumin and turmeric mixture and stir thoroughly. Top with the crispy onions.

Option 1: *cucumber salad*
Prepare the cucumber salad by placing all the ingredients in a small bowl and seasoning to taste.

Option 2: *tomato purée*
To make the sauce, place a saucepan over moderate heat and add the oil and onion. Cook until the onion is soft. Add the garlic and sauté for 2 minutes. Stir in the tomato purée and *baharat* and season to taste. Simmer for 5 minutes over low heat.

Serve *Mjederra* in bowls and allow each person to top with the tomato purée or cucumber salad as desired.

**Baharat* is a mixture of black pepper, coriander seeds, cinnamon, cloves, cumin, cardamom, nutmeg, and paprika. See *baharat* recipe on page 78.

HOTEL
or Families
0797654041
قطايف أبو علي
الشهيرة الممتازة
صيفاً شتاءً يرحب بكم
ت ٤٦٣٩٥٧٢

Street art, Jebal al-Weibdeh, Amman.

UM SAMIR

home: Homs, Syria
far from home since 2013

أم سمير

STORY TARYN LAMMI & NICOLE LAVEZZARI | **PHOTOGRAPHY** KATRINA FLETT GULBRANDSEN

"This is the only gold I have left."

Um Samir ushers us into a small room in her home — it serves as both living room and workspace. We place ourselves comfortably on cushions. She brings out two bowls filled with mixed nuts, and pulls the *soba* closer for warmth. Um Samir's well-used sewing machine sits on a table, and a pile of cloth spills across the floor. "The neighbours ask me to make them things," she declares, proudly showing us the latest piece she is working on. "If it wasn't for my skills, we wouldn't survive."

"I had an idyllic childhood," she continues, "I played and went to parks. My mother was a great encouragement to me — instead of having me clean the house, she would often tell me to go ahead and sew, or to make her something." Because of her mother's nurturing, Um Samir became a very talented seamstress. Her sister and brother-in-law took note of this and helped her open her own sewing business.

"I married when I was twenty-three. My husband and I were very disciplined in saving money. We were able to buy ourselves a home, then a second, and then even a third. We finally felt that we were well prepared for our future and the future of our children. But that is when the trouble all began."

As the conflict in Syria grew, their once-secure situation shifted dramatically. On several occasions soldiers invaded Um Samir's home, making wild accusations against the family, looking for gold, and taking what they wanted. One time, seven men came in at once. One of the men turned sharply to Um Samir and said, 'If I had come in here by myself, you all would have slaughtered me, cut me up in pieces, and put me in the refrigerator. You people are terrorists!'

Um Samir tells us, she was compelled to defend her family's honour, replying to the man, 'If anyone so much as got a cut on their finger in our home, we would be upset.'

The violence only increased over time. "Because of the danger outside our four walls, I couldn't visit my daughter who lived nearby with her husband. I couldn't even go and get bread," Um Samir explains. If you went outside you could be hit by a *qunbula*. In one explosion, shrapnel hit Um Samir's son in the eye.

Um Samir and her husband left Homs so their son could have eye surgery. The first operation was not successful, and he needed a second. Ultimately, he lost the eye. As they were returning home to Homs, "the city was completely surrounded, and there was no way in." The only option they saw was to leave Syria and make the dangerous night-time journey to Jordan. They hoped once there, registered as refugees, they could look for medical care and begin the process of applying for resettlement in another country.

Um Samir and her husband left their home, their possessions, and all their well-planned investments behind when they left for Jordan. But their four children were in danger, and so they gave everything up to try to keep them safe.

As Um Samir comes to the end of her story, I ask, "Were you able to bring anything with you out of Syria?" She replies, "I brought my gold jewelry, but we sold that to pay for the first few months of rent here." She motions to her ears, "This is the only gold I have left."

All their years of hard work and only a single pair of gold earrings remains. But there is no bitterness in her voice — quite the opposite — there is only gratitude that her family is alive and still together.

KNAFEH JIBNE

(shredded sweet pastry with cheese)

Despite her family's tragic losses, Um Samir continues to make *knafeh* — a sweet, dense pastry usually prepared to mark the sweet events of life. Um Samir's rich, citrussy recipe is a dessert to remember.

Serves: 10 - 12

INGREDIENTS:

375g (13 oz) *kunafa* pastry (available from Middle Eastern supermarkets) or substitute the Greek version, *kataifi* pastry

185g (7 oz or ¾ cup) butter, melted

375g (13 oz or 1 ½ cups) ricotta cheese, or mozzarella cheese

1 tablespoon sugar

grated zest of 1 lemon

SUGAR SYRUP:

500g (1 lb 2 oz or 1 ½ cups) sugar

1 teaspoon lemon juice

1 - 2 tablespoons rosewater or orange blossom water

500ml water (17 fl oz or 2 cups)

METHOD:

Preheat the oven to 180°C (350°F/Gas 4).

Tease apart the pastry gently with your fingers. Place in a large bowl with the melted butter and mix until the pastry shreds are evenly coated.

Place half the pastry mix in a 25 x 30cm (10 x 12-inch) baking dish, or in a 25cm (10-inch) round baking dish. Flatten down to make the pastry layer more compact.

Combine the cheese, sugar, and lemon zest in a mixing bowl and beat until softened. Add the mixture to the baking dish and spread evenly. Top with the remaining pastry.

Bake for 45 minutes, or until golden brown.

Meanwhile, for the syrup, bring the water and sugar to a boil in a heavy-based saucepan over medium heat, stirring occasionally. Add the lemon juice and simmer, without stirring, for 12 minutes, or until the syrup has thickened.

Add rosewater or orange blossom water to taste, then boil for another minute before removing from the heat. When cool, the consistency should be similar to thin honey.

Remove the *knafeh* from the oven and pour the sugar syrup over it. Leave it to cool a little, then serve warm, cut in squares, or in diamond shapes.

Store any remaining *knafeh* or syrup, covered, in the refrigerator. Leftovers can be reheated in the microwave or oven.

PALESTINIAN EMBROIDERY tatreez

with Faatima

Faatima gently unfolds the aged, fraying fabric to reveal a collection of small, hand-stitched motifs. Colourful flowers and delicate leaves are interspersed with geometric designs and snippets of beautifully designed border pattern. Some are complete, some half formed, and some seem to have been barely started before the needle was set down in favour of some new endeavour. "This work is from my mother; they are her samples from many years ago in Palestine. She was a very skilled embroiderer."

Palestinians are well-known throughout the Middle East for their skill and creativity in producing cross-stitched embroidery for the decoration of clothing and homewares. The *thobe,* or ankle-length traditional Arab dress, is today still hand embroidered and proudly worn by women for weddings and other special occasions. A *thobe* will often be richly decorated with embroidered front panel, sleeves, borders, and stripes (or branches) that extend down to the hem of the garment. A highly treasured *thobe* can be handed down within a family.

For Palestinian women, the ancient art of *tatreez* is strongly linked to their cultural belonging, regional identity, and personal history. Local varieties of the craft have been passed down from mother to daughter for generations. In the past, choices of fabric, colour, design, and method were tied to a specific region. Due to displacement and population mobility, many designs have intermingled and evolved into eclectic styles. Machine-embroidered designs are available and very popular in the Middle East, but hand-stitched *tatreez* remains a cherished and deeply-meaningful craft.

Faatima explains her family's *tatreez* tradition. "My mother taught me to embroider the traditional way when I was in sixth grade. I have nine daughters and three sons. All my daughters can sew. I really enjoy embroidering. We usually do this at night; the women and I get together when the kids are asleep and the housework is done."

For many Palestinian refugees and expatriates, *tatreez* has become an invaluable, tangible link to their lost homeland — a symbol of Palestinian pride and resilience. It is a reminder of a way of life lost, and therefore its preservation has become highly important.

Although the craft is less commonly practiced amongst the younger generation, some women's cooperatives teach the craft and adapt it for contemporary style and usage. This provides refugee and rural women with an income, while helping to preserve rich cultural traditions.

"Now I work for a local cooperative," Faatima says. "The money I receive from the work is very important to my family. We copy traditional designs we like, or we search on the internet for new designs... Mostly, we work on black fabric with one colour — I like this the best."

STORY & PHOTOGRAPHY KATRINA FLETT GULBRANDSEN

MAKE IT:

Palestinian-style cross stitch

The three embroidery charts provided on the right are inspired by traditional Palestinian *tatreez* designs, including some of Faatima's mother's motifs. The completed embroideries can be made into wall hangings, sewed or glued onto cards, or appliquéd onto clothing or other textiles.

YOU WILL NEED:

Aida cloth, at least 20 x 20cm (8 x 8 inches), 11 stitch count

embroidery thread (floss), your choice of colours

embroidery hoop, 14cm (5.5 inches)

embroidery/tapestry needle

scissors

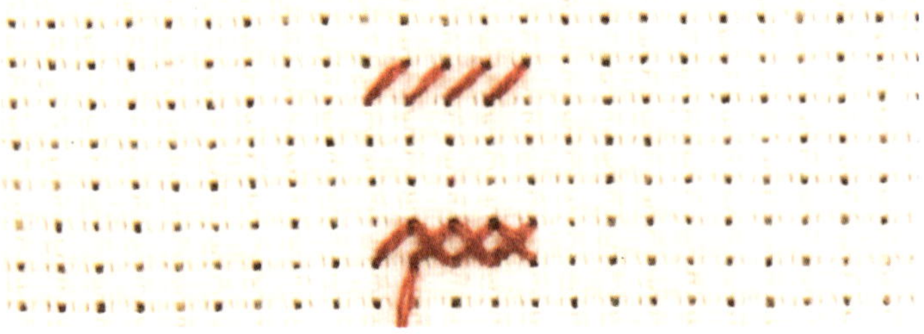

PROCESS:

1. Cut your Aida cloth. Each small square on the cloth marks the space for one cross stitch. If you are using a different stitch count Aida, count your pattern's width and length and cut the fabric accordingly.
2. To find the midpoint of the cloth, fold in half and press down to make a crease. Fold the fabric in half again and press down to make a second crease perpendicular to the first. Open the fabric to find where the creases intersect and mark with a pin.
3. Stretch the fabric across the embroidery hoop and tighten into place.
4. Cut approximately 60cm (24 inches) of embroidery thread. Take two strands.
5. Thread your needle with the two strands, leaving the end un-knotted.
6. Familiarise yourself with your chosen embroidery chart. Each square indicates one full cross and is marked with a suggested thread colour.
7. Begin your cross stitch. Most embroiderers typically begin in the centre of the design. Count the number of squares on the pattern to find the centre stitch. Insert your needle up through the fabric in the bottom left corner of the centre square. Leave a couple of centimetres (about an inch) of thread at the back.
8. Cross stitch is usually worked in horizontal rows. From the bottom left corner of a square, cross to the top right corner. Insert your needle and pull the thread down through the cloth. Work these diagonal stitches in horizontal rows, following your chart. Make sure the first few stitches cross the loose end-thread at the back to secure it to the cloth, to avoid the embroidery unravelling.

   When you have completed the row from left to right, work back along the row from right to left, crossing the stitches.

   Note: It doesn't really matter if you start your cross stitch going '////' or '\\\\' as long as you are consistent with your pattern.

   When you run out of thread or need to change thread colour, run the thread through a few stitches at the back to secure it. Cut, separate, and thread a new 2-strand piece. Run the new strands under a few stitches at the back before bringing the thread through to the front and continuing to stitch.
9. When you have completed the pattern, run the remaining thread under a few stitches at the back. Cut off the remaining thread.

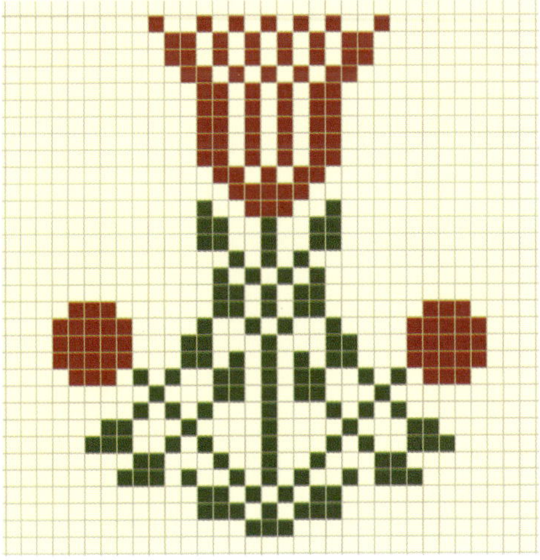

Aida cloth: Aida is a loosely woven cloth in a grid pattern that comes in a range of stitch counts. It is easiest to start on an Aida cloth that uses an 11-stitch count, as this provides larger spaces for your cross stitch. The higher the stitch count, the smaller your crosses will be.

Embroidery thread: This usually comes in 6 strands. To separate the strands, gently pull apart the thread from the centre of the piece. You will use 2 strands for these patterns.

SELVA
home: Aleppo, Syria
far from home since 2012

سيلفا

STORY SALLY BATHGATE | **PHOTOGRAPHY** WILMA STEENBEEK

"Our life was so great in Aleppo... I was always surrounded by family."

Our two families sit together in the simple living room, East and West meeting together, eating together. We savour desserts to mark the occasion of Selva moving to a new house, a bittersweet experience born of necessity rather than choice. It is the fourth or fifth home Selva's family has lived in since fleeing from Syria to Jordan — although their situation is perhaps more stable than that of many other refugee families.

Selva's family reminisces about better days in Aleppo, which sounds, to our ears, like paradise on earth.

"Our life was so great in Aleppo," Selva says. "There were no problems. It was simple, and I was always surrounded by family. I particularly loved visiting family, especially at *Eid*; wearing new dresses, going here and there – it was perfect.

"As kids, my mother always bought us new clothes and pampered us. School life was delightful. I had many friends, and like most children, we played and made mischief more than we studied. I finished school at grade nine. After that I started helping Mum with housework. She insisted on that so that I would become a good housewife. I had a number of men proposing marriage but none of them was suitable until I saw Waseem. Waseem came along, and we were engaged. After one-and-a-half years, we were married."

She describes her wedding day, before the war began:

"In the early morning, I went to the salon, then I went home and put on my wedding dress. All Waseem's family came to my family home in a great procession of cars, honking their horns and flashing their lights — what we call a *zafeh*. Once outside, all of them sang and beat drums. My eleven uncles stood in a line with my brothers and my sisters' husbands, and I passed between them, shaking hands with every one of them, until I finally reached the street. Once outside there was dancing and music with all the guests.

"Next we went to the wedding hall, a place outside the city in the beautiful countryside, for the wedding party. The celebration was mixed, men and women together, since we were all relatives. A giant cake was brought for the cake show, and we cut it with a sword. We celebrated until one in the morning. After that we left for our new home."

We watch the video of the wedding, one of the few things the family have brought with them to Jordan. They are relaxed and happy in the pictures on screen, hands joined all together as they dance a traditional *dabkeh*. Then Waseem and his father point out each family member in turn. "They are in Germany... This uncle is in Russia... She is in Turkey..." and so on. The family is scattered to the ends of the earth, with only Selva's parents and a sister holding on in Syria, in a village two hours from Aleppo.

Selva explains, "My parents and sister used to live in the city, but after the war began, their house was stolen. So they decided to move to a rural area. They live as if in the past. For example, my mum washes by hand and cooks using firewood. But my mum has asthma and she spends most of her time at the doctor's clinic."

My husband, Ben, opens a satellite photo map on his phone to see a bird's-eye view of Selva and Waseem's neighbourhood in Aleppo as it looks now, three years after their departure from Syria. It is a mess of collapsed concrete buildings. Their home, their neighbourhood — is rubble.

"Our life in Aleppo was better than here in Jordan," Selva says. "We are feeling sad, but at the same time, we are much better off than others because neither we nor our children died in the war, *Alhamdulillah*. Our life was simple, inexpensive, with everything available; we hope our country recovers and the war ends."

KOUSA MAHSHI BI BANDOURA

(stuffed zucchini with tomato)

"Do you like *kousa mahshi*?" Selva's mother-in-law asks expectantly. Not all *kousa mahshi* are created equal, but with Selva's flavourful recipe, it is safe to answer, "Yes!" and enjoy a plateful.

Serves: 6 - 8 as a main course

INGREDIENTS:

2kg (4 lb 6 oz) evenly sized zucchini (courgettes), small or medium in size

2L (68 fl oz or 8 cups) water

6 tablespoons tomato paste

8 cloves of garlic, crushed or minced

2 teaspoons dried mint

1 tablespoon tamarind paste

Salt and freshly ground black pepper, to season

STUFFING

450g (1 lb or 2 cups) short-grain white rice, soaked in water for 15 minutes

1 tablespoon ghee or oil

200g (7 oz) minced (ground) lamb or beef

½ teaspoon cumin

½ teaspoon turmeric

1 teaspoon salt

freshly ground black pepper, to season

METHOD:

Wash the zucchini well. Cut off the stem end of the zucchini. Using a vegetable or apple corer*, hollow out each zucchini, leaving the rounded end intact. Try not to puncture the skin. Rinse out any remaining scraps.

Wash the rice and drain in a sieve. Place the rice and the remaining stuffing ingredients into a bowl. Season with pepper and thoroughly combine.

Fill the zucchini with the stuffing.

Arrange the zucchini in layers in a heavy-based saucepan, sprinkling the layers lightly with salt. In a separate bowl, mix the 2L (68 fl oz or 8 cups) of water with the tomato paste and stir to combine. Pour this broth over the zucchini, and add the garlic, tamarind, and mint. Invert a heavy plate on top of the zucchini and bring to a slow simmer. Cover and simmer gently for 40 - 45 minutes, or until tender.

When cooked, carefully remove the plate from the broth. Using a slotted spoon, remove the zucchini and serve on a large, flat plate. Pour the broth into a large bowl to accompany the meal. Serve with flatbread and a side salad.

*Middle Eastern food suppliers usually stock a special corer for preparing vegetables for stuffing. It is not as wide as an apple corer and much longer.

لوز مقشور مالح
لوز فرك مالح
الوقية
٣,٠٠٠ د
250

MA'MOUL

(nut or date filled biscuits)

Ma'moul is the Middle Eastern biscuit of festival time. Selva and her family prepare a nut-filled variety of these pastries to celebrate the end of *Ramadan (Eid al-Fitr)* and the end of the performance of the yearly pilgrimage to Mecca (*Eid al-Adha*).

Ma'moul also feature during Christian holidays — Christmas and especially Easter feasts would not be complete without a plateful of sugar-dusted *ma'moul* among the desserts.

Makes: About 60

INGREDIENTS:

DOUGH

700g (1 lb 9 oz or 4 cups) fine semolina*

250g (9 oz or 1 cup) butter, softened

75g (3 oz or ⅓ cup) sugar

75ml (2 ½ fl oz or ⅓ cup) water

OPTION 1 - nut filling

165g (6 oz or ¾ cup) caster sugar

180ml (6 fl oz or ¾ cup) water

400g (14 oz) pistachio or walnut, ground to coarse crumbs

½ teaspoon cinnamon

1 teaspoon rosewater

OPTION 2 - date filling**

1kg (2 lb 3 oz) of pitted soft dates

1 teaspoon cinnamon

1 teaspoon ground anise

1 teaspoon ground cardamom

2 tablespoons melted butter

Optional garnish: powdered sugar for sprinkling on the finished biscuits. Selva prefers *ma'moul* without the extra sugar. However, some bakers don't consider *ma'moul* to be complete without it.

METHOD:

In a large mixing bowl, combine the semolina and butter, and mix well. Add the water and sugar and form into a dough, kneading lightly. Allow the dough to rest, tightly covered with cling film, at room temperature, for an hour or more.

For the nut filling, combine all the ingredients in a bowl until everything sticks together.

Alternatively, for the date filling, use a mortar and pestle or a food processor to grind the ingredients into a thick paste. Roll this paste into small balls — small enough to fit inside a walnut-sized ball of dough.

Preheat the oven to 230°C (450°F/Gas 8).

Knead the dough again to make it pliable. Roll a tablespoonful of dough into a ball the size of a large walnut. Repeat with the remaining mixture. Flatten a ball in your palm, then push up the sides to make a bowl. Fill the hollow with a heaped teaspoon of filling, or a date ball, and close the dough over the filing, pressing the edges to seal. Roll into a ball again and place onto a tray lined with baking paper. Repeat for the remaining balls. Flatten the balls slightly with a fork.

Alternatively, you may shape the biscuits using a *tabi,* a decoratively carved mould used in traditional biscuit making. Place the balls into the mould and tap out on a board, then transfer the shaped biscuits to a tray lined with baking paper.

Place the biscuits in the oven, reduce the oven temperature to 180°C (350°F/Gas 4), and bake for 20 - 25 minutes.

When cool, sprinkle with powdered sugar, if desired, and store in an airtight container.

*Fine semolina can be purchased from Middle Eastern grocery stores or specialty supermarkets.

**Alternatively, ready-made date paste can be found in any Middle Eastern market.

A wedding celebration spills out into the street, Jebal al-Hussein, Amman.

WARID

home: Homs, Syria
far from home since 2013

ورد

STORY NICOLE LAVEZZARI | **PHOTOGRAPHY** KATRINA FLETT GULBRANDSEN

"... once the war started and we had to leave our country, I felt I had to leave my dreams there too."

"I have always wanted to be a beautician," Warid tells us as she glides into her living room with a tray of elaborately crafted desserts. She has an eye for beauty and an appreciation for detail. Everything about the young woman's appearance is breathtaking. She has taken great care with her wardrobe, makeup, and hair. She moves with confidence and elegance.

"My father owned a bridal wear shop back in Syria," she continues, "and I dreamed of opening a beauty parlor next door — to do the bride's hair, nails, makeup, and henna. However, once the war started and we had to leave our country, I felt I had to leave my dreams there too."

Warid's family escaped to Jordan when she was sixteen, and the attractive girl was quickly noticed. Before long, eligible bachelors were showing up at her door. "Young men would follow me home from school every day," she says. Warid was so unsettled by the attention, she pretended to be sick for a week just so she could stay home and avoid her admirers. "I didn't want people to get the wrong idea about my character."

Her parents felt she was too young to marry but still allowed suitors to come, always warning that they were not looking for a husband for her. "I had suitors from several different countries, but I wanted to marry someone from the area where I grew up, someone who could relate to my life before."

One day, they were approached by a man from her hometown. Warid liked him, and so they started to get to know each other. They were allowed to sit next to each other and talk in one corner of the room, while their mothers chaperoned. Through this process, they found that they were well suited to one another. It was clear to both families that this engagement wouldn't just be an arrangement; it was truly love. Around a year later, they were happily married.

Warid's childhood dream, while deferred, has not disappeared. She still longs to create beauty, to make other women look their loveliest on their wedding day, "for their own romance", she says. Determined to fulfill her dreams, and with the support of her husband and mother, she is working towards opening a business in her home.

Soon after dessert and her story, I become one of her first clients. In her expert hands I receive a glamorous, Syrian-style makeover, complete with a voluminous new hair style and dramatic makeup. "Your husband won't even recognize you!" she says, with a smile of pride at a successful transformation.

MUHALLABIA

(almond and vanilla milk pudding)

Like her makeup and henna designs, Warid's assorted desserts are intricate works of art. Raspberry red jelly and creamy yellow custard are layered carefully in dessert glasses and topped with sliced bananas. Sliced fruit is meticulously arranged on large plates in elegant, colourful designs. One of her favourite desserts is *muhallabia*, a popular vanilla milk pudding. Warid says that *muhallabia* can be set in the refrigerator, or may be eaten warm. It is easy to make, sweet, and delicious!

Serves: 6

INGREDIENTS:

35g (1 ¼ oz or ¼ cup) rice flour

750ml (25 fl oz or 3 cups) milk

pinch of salt

55g (2 oz or ¼ cup) sugar

80g (3 oz or ¾ cup) ground almonds

1 teaspoon vanilla essence

pistachios or almonds, to serve

pomegranate seeds, to serve (optional)

METHOD:

Mix the rice flour in 185ml (6 ½ fl oz or ¾ cup) of the milk.

Bring the remaining milk to a boil in a saucepan, then stir in the rice flour mixture, salt, and sugar.

Using medium heat, stir constantly with a wooden spoon until the mixture bubbles gently.

Reduce the heat and simmer gently for 5 minutes, stirring often. It is important that the mixture cooks slowly.

Stir in the ground almonds until combined and smooth. Add the vanilla and remove from the heat.

Stir occasionally while the mixture cools, then pour into 6 individual ramekins or small bowls (about ½ cup of mixture for each ramekin/bowl).

Chill the puddings and serve garnished with nuts, and pomegranate seeds if available.

SYRIAN-STYLE HENNA al hinna

with Warid

Warid's gold bangles sparkle and clang together as she grips Nicole's arm. She concentrates intently and her hand is steady. Warid's other guests sit back and relax on well-worn mattresses, stomachs full and more than satisfied. We watch the swirling design form. Warid is in her element. Like most traditional henna artists from Syria, Warid specialises in floral motifs. Swirling and curling from the finger tips, lines, vines, and petals wrap the wrist and stretch up Nicole's forearm.

The English word henna comes from the Arabic word *al hinna* and can refer to the henna plant (*Lawsonia Inermis*) as well as the red-brown dye produced by grinding the leaves, stems, and flowers of the plant into a fine powder.

For thousands of years in the Middle East, henna powder has been used for household dying and cosmetic purposes, including skin decoration. The use of henna to decorate the skin is associated with special celebrations. These include engagements, weddings, births, and religious festivals. The style, purpose, spiritual significance, and meaning can vary greatly by tribe or region.

Middle Eastern women today still use henna to dye their hair and skin. Women apply henna to each other in the privacy of their own homes, visit a beauty parlour, or have a professional artist come to an arranged henna party. Many brides will have a henna celebration before the wedding. A typical party will include a bride's female friends and relatives, an abundance of food, dancing, and very loud music!

STORY & PHOTOGRAPHY KATRINA FLETT GULBRANDSEN

DO IT:

henna body art

Try the provided patterns inspired by traditional Syrian designs, or create your own!

YOU WILL NEED:

a henna cone — Ready-made cones are the easiest and most practical way for a beginner to apply henna. Henna can be bought online and at speciality shops. It also comes in raw powdered form. If you choose to mix your own henna, follow the instructions on the box.

tissues

alcohol wipes or warm water and soap

plastic wrap

henna body art continued on next page

SAFETY TIPS:

When mixing and/or applying henna, always follow the instructions and warnings on the packaging, and protect other skin and surfaces from contact with the dye.

Natural henna is a very safe substance; however, if you are concerned about an adverse reaction to the dye, do a small skin patch test first.

Ready-mixed henna mixtures can contain harmful additives to alter the colour of the dye. Natural and safe henna will always be shades of red-brown, not black.

If you spill the henna, or make a mistake, wash it off immediately.

PROCESS:

Applying henna using a cone:

1. Clean the skin with water and soap or wipe with an alcohol wipe. Make sure no soap residue remains on the skin.
2. Choose your design and familiarise yourself with the pattern. If you prefer a little guidance as you apply the henna, use a water soluble marker or pen and draw your design onto the skin. The henna can be applied directly over the top.
3. Hold the cone firmly in your palm with the pointed end between your thumb and pointer finger. For maximum control and consistency, gently squeeze the tube with your palm and fingers from the back of the tube. You will need to find a position that is comfortable for you. Some artists use their other hand to help support the cone, or lean their drawing hand down onto their little finger to keep the application steady; it will get easier with practice.

After application:

4. Cover the henna with tissue and then wrap in plastic wrap. Leave for at least 5 hours or overnight. The heat and moisture retention will help the dye to mature and deepen. The plastic will also keep the henna paste on the skin for as long as possible — the longer the contact, the darker and longer lasting the colour will be.
5. Carefully remove the plastic and tissue. Pull off any remaining henna paste. Use a little olive oil (rather than water) if the paste gets stuck to the skin. At first the henna may be a lighter shade of orange/brown, but it should darken over time. The henna design may last anywhere between 3 days and 3 weeks, depending on the henna quality, application, maturation time, skin type, and location of application.

Tips for keeping the henna design longer:

- Avoid contact with water for the first 24 hours
- Cover the henna design with a little olive oil before showering or swimming
- Avoid rubbing or shaving over the area

Oliva

UM GHASAN home: Homs, Syria far from home since 2013

أم غسان

STORY NICOLE LAVEZZARI | **PHOTOGRAPHY** KATRINA FLETT GULBRANDSEN

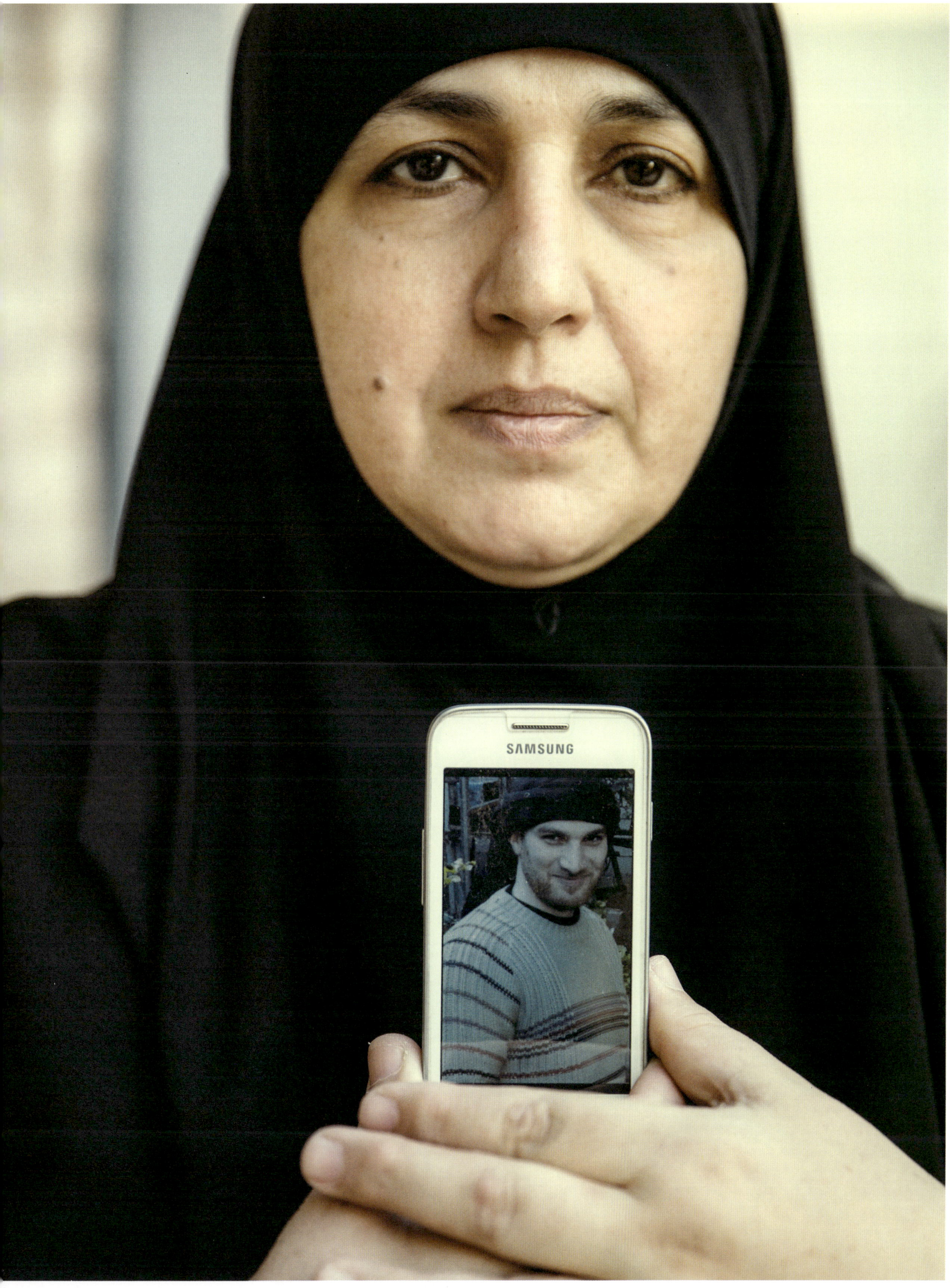
SAMSUNG

"First he worked as an activist, and then he helped bring medical supplies to those who were injured..."

"From the beginning, our neighborhood saw violence and killing," Um Ghasan tells us. "At the time, my son Ahmed was a student at the university, in religious studies. While studying, he learned that it was part of his duty to God to join the war. So very early on, he joined the Free Syrian Army. First he worked as an activist, and then he helped bring medical supplies to those who were injured. Then, as the war progressed, he would make the dangerous trip to Lebanon to get weapons so our people could defend themselves. Finally, he was elevated to the high position of judge.

"While he remained to do his part in the war, the rest of our family felt we needed to leave. My youngest son left for Jordan soon after the trouble started. There was so much trouble. There were tanks outside shooting the buildings randomly; we had to stay in interior rooms, away from the windows. We finally decided to leave after a bombardment caused the wall of our house to fall in on us. The day after we left our house, the government forces came in and started killing people, even young children! We never went back to our home after that.

"We became refugees inside our own country, going from place to place. All the people of our neighbourhood ended up like that. After four months, my son who had traveled to Jordan told us to come. We came across the border illegally, just my daughter and I. We walked at night through mine fields to the border. From there we rode in a van, but the government forces realised we were there and started shooting at us; we could feel the bullets go by. We made it safely, and not too long after that, my husband came.

"We didn't bring anything with us, just ourselves and the clothes we were wearing. I have cried so much for all the things we had to leave, our house was filled with things. I couldn't even bring my gold; we fled with just our lives.

"But none of that matters now... My son Ahmed is dead. He never once shot a gun, but he was killed by a sniper."

It has been more than a year since she heard the news. On that day, in the desert town where she had sought refuge, she was joined by other refugee women in her grief. The room was full of women sitting on mats on the ground. The mood was heavy and tense, shrouded by the whispers of a few women praying. The coffee served was bitter; it was a bitter occasion. Um Ghasan sobbed uncontrollably. Some of the women tried to comfort her, "He was a martyr — your family is guaranteed a place in heaven."

Um Ghasan gripped her phone, debating whether to look at it or not. She faced a torturous dilemma. On it was a picture of her son, after his death. Should she look at it to confirm that her son was really dead? Or should she not, so that she could remember him as he was in life?

Unravelled by grief, Um Ghasan was paralysed by the impossible decision she had to make. But she had to know — to see for herself, whatever the cost.

In a hasty, protective move, her daughter grabbed the phone and told her not to look, urging her mother to remember him as he was. Um Ghasan's daughter deleted the picture. It had been over a year since Um Ghasan had seen him... and now she would never see him again.

It has taken her a long time to find the courage to share her story. She remembers him proudly, in his youthful idealism and service to their beloved country. "His picture was shown on Syrian television; he was a war hero.

"I still feel like he is alive with us. Since his death, my husband and I continue to have dreams of him. Every time I have a dream of him, he is giving me something; then the very next day, there is some sort of provision for us."

With tears in her eyes, she shows again the video clip of her son being honoured.

A Jordanian desert village close to the Syrian border.

MAQLOUBE

(upside-down chicken and vegetable pilaf)

Um Ghasan's *maqloube* is a hearty, complete meal — the flavours and textures of the meat, vegetables, and rice meld into a towering mound of goodness. Much of the enjoyment of this dish is in its visual appeal. Many home cooks in the Middle East enhance the presentation of their dishes by adding a creative flourish. Feel free to layer the rice, meat, and vegetables as it pleases you, and garnish with flair.

Serves: 6 - 8

INGREDIENTS:

POACHED CHICKEN

1 chicken, cut into 6 pieces

1 large brown onion, sliced

1 cinnamon stick, broken in half

2 bay leaves

3 whole cardamom pods, slightly crushed

1 teaspoon allspice berries*

PILAF

oil, for frying

1 eggplant (aubergine), cut into 1cm (½ inch)-thick rounds

1 small cauliflower, cut into small florets

1 small onion, finely diced

500g (1 lb 2 oz) lean minced lamb

2 teaspoons *garam masala*

sea salt and freshly ground black pepper

¼ teaspoon ground cinnamon

750g (1 lb 11 oz) long-grain rice, rinsed well and cooked

TO SERVE

pine nuts, lightly toasted

slivered almonds, lightly toasted

yoghurt

parsley

METHOD:

Place the chicken, onion, herbs, and spices in a large saucepan with enough water to just cover. Bring to a boil over high heat, then reduce the heat to low and simmer gently for 40 minutes or until the chicken is completely tender. Remove the chicken and reserve the stock.

When the chicken is cool enough to handle, remove and discard the skin and bones, and shred the meat roughly into largish pieces.

Meanwhile, heat the oil in a large frypan. Cook the eggplant and cauliflower, in batches, for 3 - 4 minutes or until golden. Remove with a slotted spoon and drain on a paper towel. Remove all but 1 teaspoon of the oil.

Using the same frypan, sauté the onion gently for 5 minutes. Increase the heat, add the lamb, and sauté until the juices evaporate. Add the *garam masala*, cinnamon, and a large pinch of salt and stir well.

Line the base of a 6L (200 fl oz)-capacity, non-stick saucepan with the eggplant. Spread about one third of the cooked rice over the top, then sprinkle half the lamb mixture over the rice, and season to taste with salt and pepper. Press each layer tightly into the pan as you work. Place the chicken on the top, followed by the cauliflower. Sprinkle the remaining lamb mixture over the cauliflower, and season again. Cover with the remaining rice so that it comes to about 2.5cm (1 inch) below the top of the pan.

Pour over enough of the stock to just cover the layered ingredients. Cover with a lid and simmer over the lowest possible heat until the stock is absorbed, or 20 minutes maximum. To serve: place a tray or platter tightly over the top of the pan, invert the pan by flipping it over away from yourself, and tap sharply several times to loosen the contents before lifting off the pan. Sprinkle the toasted nuts and parsley on top. Serve immediately with a side of yoghurt.

*allspice berries (pimento) can be purchased from Middle Eastern grocery stores

SAMIRA & FAMILY

home: Daraa', Syria
far from home since 2013

سميرة و العائلة

STORY JONATHAN MORGAN | **PHOTOGRAPHY** KATRINA FLETT GULBRANDSEN

"Do they have cats in Australia?"

"Do they have cats in Australia?"

We've just arrived at Samira's home and her youngest son, Mohammed, walks through the door with a new kitten he's just bought. The family are ecstatic.

"We used to have a white cat in Daraa' but had to leave everything behind. We had a white dog too."

The family are hard-working farming folk who love animals and the countryside.

They are excited to find out that Australia is considering their resettlement application.

Raif, the eldest son, like many Syrians, loves birds. "I've heard that in Australia there are parrots of all different colours and sizes, big and small!"

Anne, who comes from Australia, pulls out her phone and shows him pictures of rosellas. "These are common in Australia," she tells him.

Raif is excited. "That's the biggest thing I'm looking forward to, the birds! My mum's excited about the Australian food, and Marianna can't wait to start studying. But I really just want to see all the birds."

His phone rings. It's a client interested in buying some of his canaries.

The South African grey parrot eyes the new kitten nervously as it scampers past its cage.

Samira's family arrived in Jordan four years ago and have applied for the UNHCR resettlement program through our NGO, which advocates for refugees, helping them to communicate with agencies like the UNHCR and the Australian Embassy. Refugees are expected to complete detailed application forms during the process, all in English. NGOs like ours offer free translation services, as well as checking the status of applications that have been submitted.

Over a cup of green tea, Samira explains the meal she's prepared for us tonight:

"We served this at our wedding. It's one of my favourite dishes. It's like the Jordanian dish, *mansaf*, but with bulgur wheat instead of rice, and a sauce that isn't sour."

Faaris, the middle son, talks about the thriving industries that existed in Syria before the war. "We didn't need to import much, because what we needed, we grew or made. We made our own clothes, grew our own vegetables, and reared our own livestock. Here in Jordan, all the meat is imported, but in Syria we had locally sourced meat."

We tell them about some of the meat that is unique to Australia and a new discussion emerges:

"Is kangaroo meat *haram* or *halal*?"

After some discussion about what type of claws kangaroos have, and a quick internet search, Faaris comes back smiling:

"Kangaroos are *halal*! I'm ready to barbecue!"

MANSAF

(lamb and yoghurt pilaf)

Mansaf is considered the national dish of Jordan, serving as the equivalent of the Sunday roast as well as the dish of choice at big feasts. Samira and her family, coming from nearby Daraa', make a Syrian version of *mansaf*, serving the meat — lamb or chicken — with burghul instead of rice. The signature ingredient of *mansaf* is *jameed*. This dehydrated, fermented, salted yoghurt is formed into balls that can be stored for long periods at room temperature. It can be found in selected Middle Eastern grocers.

Serves: 8

INGREDIENTS:

half a ball of *jameed*, or substitute with 250g (9 oz or 1 cup) of plain yoghurt

900g (32 oz or 3 ½ cups) plain yoghurt

2 cups warm water

2 tablespoons ghee or vegetable oil

2kg (4 ½ lbs) lamb shoulder on the bone — ask your butcher to cut it into 8 evenly-sized pieces, or substitute lamb shoulder chops

1 medium onion, chopped

½ teaspoon allspice

½ teaspoon turmeric

2 bay leaves

1 small cinnamon stick

salt and pepper, to taste

400g (14 oz or 2 cups) burghul (also known as bulgur)

750ml (8 ½ fl oz or 3 cups) hot water

FOR SERVING

1 cup nuts, toasted (use pine nuts, slivered almonds or halved peanuts, as preferred)

½ cup chopped parsley

2 flatbreads (recipe p. 142)

METHOD:

If you are using *jameed*, crush it into small chunks and soak it in 2 cups of warm water for about an hour prior to starting the cooking process. You might need to leave it overnight if the *jameed* is very hard.

Melt the ghee or oil in a large saucepan, and brown the lamb. Remove the lamb and fry the onion on medium heat until soft. Return the lamb to the saucepan and add sufficient hot water to cover the meat. Add the allspice, turmeric, bay leaves, cinnamon stick, and salt and pepper to taste. Bring to a boil over high heat. Reduce the heat to medium and simmer, uncovered, for 1 hour or until the meat is almost falling off the bone.

When the meat is almost ready, prepare the burghul. In a small saucepan, combine the burghul, water, and salt. Bring to a boil. Add a ladle or two of the meat broth to the burghul for extra flavour. Reduce heat to medium and cook for 20 - 30 minutes, stirring occasionally. Add more boiling water if required.

Next, if you are using *jameed*, blend it with its soaking water into a smooth liquid, strain it, and pour it into a large saucepan — large enough to eventually hold 6 - 7 cups of liquid plus all of the meat.

Add the yoghurt (3 ½ cups if using *jameed*, 4 ½ cups if not using *jameed*) to the saucepan and heat it over medium heat, stirring continuously, until it boils. It is important to stir continuously to prevent the yoghurt from curdling. Lower the heat and add the meat, along with 2 - 3 ladlefuls of the meat broth. Adjust the consistency with extra broth or water, stirring until you have a thin, soup-like mixture. Simmer until all the flavours have combined.

Line a serving platter with split flatbread. Pile on the burghul and cover with the lamb pieces and a few ladlefuls of the yoghurt soup. Garnish with nuts and parsley and serve with the remaining yoghurt soup in bowls on the side.

For an authentic *mansaf* experience, invite your guests to eat directly from the main platter. Each person's portion is the segment of the platter immediately in front of them, and they are free to ladle extra broth on their portion as desired.

KHOBIZ

(flatbread)

For Samira's family, bread is served at almost every meal and in between. It is the essence of life in the Middle East: inspiring folktales and proverbs. One favourite saying is *bein-na khobiz u maleh,* which means there is bread and salt between us. It is a way of saying that you are close to someone — sharing food, friendship, and loyalty.

Serves: 8

INGREDIENTS:

1 teaspoon active dried yeast

1 teaspoon salt

½ teaspoon sugar

400g (1 lb or 3 cups) plain flour, plus extra for kneading

1 tablespoon oil

250ml (8 ½ fl oz or 1 cup) warm (not hot) water

METHOD:

Dissolve the salt and sugar in the water. Add the yeast and stir. Leave for 5 minutes or so, until slightly frothy.

Stir in the flour, then add the oil gradually. Beat until smooth, either by hand for 10 minutes, or with an electric mixer using a dough hook for 5 minutes. Sprinkle some of the reserved flour onto a clean surface.

Turn out the dough and knead for 10 minutes, using more flour as required. The dough is ready when it is smooth and satiny, with a slightly wrinkled texture. Shape the dough into a ball.

Place the dough in an oiled bowl, cover with plastic wrap, and leave to rise in a warm place for 1 - 1 ½ hours, or until almost doubled in size.

Preheat the oven to 250°C (480°F/Gas 9). Keep the oven closed as much as possible during the baking of each flatbread, to maintain even heat.

Punch down the dough and turn it out onto a lightly floured work surface. Divide it into eight equal pieces, rolling each into a ball. Roll each ball into a 15cm (6-inch) circle and place on a lightly floured surface. Cover with another cloth and allow to rise for a further 10 minutes.

Heat a large baking tray on the lowest shelf of an electric oven; in a gas oven, select the section of the oven with the most even heat, probably near the top.

Oil the heated baking tray with canola spray or similar, or place the dough on a sheet of baking paper. Using a spatula, slide the first round of dough onto the tray, and quickly return it to the oven.

Bake for 4 - 5 minutes, or until the dough puffs up like a balloon.

Remove the bread from the oven and wrap it in a cloth to keep it warm and soft. Bake the remaining rounds in the same way.

Jebal al-Hussein camp, Amman, Jordan. This camp was established to accommodate Palestinian refugees who fled or were expelled from their homeland during the 1948 Arab-Israeli War. It is one of 10 Palestinian refugee camps in Jordan which continue to accommodate 370,000 Palestinians. The camps have since developed into urban structures, but continue to be afflicted by severe overcrowding and poverty. There are over 2 million registered Palestinian refugees in Jordan today.

(UNRWA - United Nations Relief and Works Agency for Palestinian Refugees in the Near East)

ARABIC CALLIGRAPHY al khat al arabi

with Faisal Afghani

"My handwriting is terrible," he says, with a wry grin. His body is bent over the well-worn counter of his family-owned antique and handicraft store in Amman, Jordan. Pencil in hand, he is creating a new design to be engraved in metal for a client.

"Seeking asylum is a part of my family's history. My grandfather was exiled from Afghanistan, and fled to Jaffa, Palestine, in 1890 to start a new life. My grandfather started the family's first store in Jaffa, naming it Alafghani. He was married and had three sons; my father and his two brothers.

"My father and mother were also refugees. They fled from Palestine to Jordan by foot with eleven other family members in 1948." This was during the Arab-Israeli War, referred to among Palestinians as *Al Nahkba* - the Catastrophe. Faisal's family left their village, along with an estimated 700,000 other Palestinians fleeing the war, or being forcibly expelled from their homes. "They left everything they had in Jaffa; including the family store. They left very quickly; it was a sad thing. They were told 'Leave everything, you can come back later.' They never did.

"My father and two uncles settled and started to work in Salt, north of Amman. They started a new store and sold soaps, bottles, things like this. My father was a goldsmith. He learnt how to engrave agate; it is a very delicate and creative craft. Their store grew little by little. I was born in Salt. In 1954, they came to Amman and established their first down-town store. We still have this store today. We now have twelve or thirteen stores in Amman... I can't remember exactly how many.

"I learnt the art of calligraphy when I was forty years old. I needed this art, I insisted on having it... to know it. Whatever you work on, you must feel it. I express my soul when I write calligraphy. When I write something using calligraphy, I must know what it is about; I must know what it means, so I can express it better. It is a rare craft now; more is done with computers these days.

"We used to make our own ink using soot and natural colourants, extracted from vegetable matter and minerals. But now, I don't have time; I'm too old. We mostly use black ink in Arabic calligraphy. Bamboo calligraphy sticks, *boosa*, are hand cut to suit the hand of the calligrapher. Every man, every hand, has its own cut. The calligrapher must feel comfortable when he writes; he himself should cut his own pen."

He leans back and reaches for a box on the shelf behind the counter. He opens it and pulls out a well-used, ink-stained bamboo calligraphy stick.

"I call this one *Aziiza* - the Dearest," he says. "When I write with this one, I feel very comfortable. I have spares of course," he smiles, "...but not another *Aziiza*."

STORY KATRINA FLETT GULBRANDSEN | **PHOTOGRAPHY** KATRINA FLETT GULBRANDSEN & BEN BATHGATE

Faisal's family stands in front of their first store in Jaffa, Palestine.

MAKE IT:

bamboo calligraphy pen

YOU WILL NEED:

a fresh bamboo stalk

garden clippers

a sharp knife

a razor blade

PROCESS:

1. Using garden clippers, cut a fresh bamboo stalk that sits comfortably in your hand. The piece should be approximately 30cm (12 inches) in length.
2. Trim off any leaves or extra branches.
3. Rest the bamboo against a work table while holding it firmly with one hand. Using a sharp knife, cut away the top of the stalk (away from the body, using a scooping motion), around 2 - 3cm (1+ inch) from the end of the bamboo. This will create the nib. You are aiming to make a 30 - 40° plane cut to the end of the stalk. Work carefully and slowly. The cut surface should be smooth and the nib slightly flexible, but not too thin.
4. Now use the knife to scrape and flatten out the last centimetre (½ inch) of the nib.
5. Next, you need to slowly trim the sides of the nib to make it the width you desire. Make a flat edge leading to the tip of the pen.
6. Using the razor blade, gently cut a small slit down the middle of the nib without cutting through to the tip — this reduces the likelihood of splitting the nib. This slit helps the pen to soak up the ink.
7. Finally, use the knife to trim the tip with one clean cut to the angle desired. You may need to experiment with different angles. Your pen is ready for use!

DO IT:

Arabic calligraphy

YOU WILL NEED:

black ink

textured card

your bamboo pen

PROCESS:

Dip the end of the nib into the ink. As you begin drawing, keep the flat nib parallel to the paper surface. You may wish to play with your pen on scrap paper to get to know the range of the nib and how to manage the ink flow before beginning your piece. The pictured calligraphy by Faisal can be copied onto your textured card to make greeting cards or art.

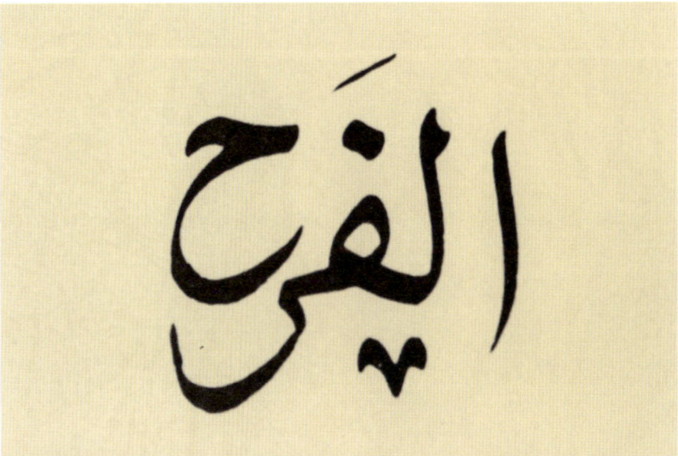

JOY *farah*

HOPE *amal*

PEACE *salam*

LOVE *hub*

A professional calligrapher, Hasan Kan'an, works in his studio in Amma

RÛLKANÊ

home: Aleppo, Syria

far from home since August 2013

STORY & PHOTOGRAPHY KATRINA FLETT GULBRANDSEN

"My father used to quote a favourite Kurdish poet, Cigerxwîn: Without learning there can be no progress."

I drove up the narrow lane, off the main road towards a house set apart on the edge of a dark, slumbering, pine forest. Rolkana had said the house was out of town. I recalled her uneasiness about living in this wild and isolated spot on the outskirts of Vennesla, Norway. What looked like the Garden of Eden to me felt lonely and alien to her. The view from her double-glazed windows was filled with the snow-white encroaching arms of the forest. She had never equated the word 'peace' with stillness and solitude.

Inside Rolkana's home, the fire and hospitality of her family warmed me. They shared laughter and tenderness; their smiling faces little indicating past trauma and continuing adversity. I looked around and saw a functional yet sparsely furnished home. Here lived a family evolving, bravely allowing an identity grounded firmly in Syria to move haltingly towards the grey stillness, traditions, and subtleties of Norway.

Rolkana and her family gathered around the large coffee table in the living room. A bowl of tabbouleh laced with sweet crimson pomegranate was placed beside a plate of spiced Christmas biscuits in the shapes of stars and hearts. A native pine, decorated with tinsel and baubles, sat in one corner of the room. To the side of the tree, on an otherwise bare wall, a single portrait hung — a man in his mid-forties with a warm smile. He was Isam, Rolkana's father.

Later, when we were alone, with tears forming in her eyes, she said, "He called to tell me he was at the border. He said, 'I'll call you again when I'm on the other side.' ... It was around six hours later when we heard the news." Her father was killed ten minutes after the phone call, in a car bombing incident as he waited to cross the border between Turkey and Syria. He left behind his wife and five children. She continues, "Until now I cannot believe it, because he was just going for a few days... I didn't see him again; we couldn't even get to the funeral... It has been over three years since that day, and I can't really believe it happened."

Rolkana is twenty-four years old. She comes from Aleppo, Syria, and is the eldest of five siblings. She was in her second year of mechatronic engineering at university in Aleppo when life became increasingly unstable and dangerous in her neighbourhood. She explained, "I couldn't go to university any more because of all the bombing... At times there was no food, no water, and no electricity. We stayed in Syria as long as we could, and then escaped to Turkey.

"My father worked in anaesthetics at Shihan Hospital in Aleppo until it became a base for regime soldiers during the war. After this he found one day of work per week at a small hospital out of the city." After settling his family in Turkey he returned to Syria to work; however, he regularly crossed the border into Turkey to be with his family, and it was these circumstances that led to his death on the 15th of May, 2014.

In Turkey, Rolkana, her sister Nazli, and their two teenaged brothers worked twelve to fifteen hours a day in a clothing factory for around three years. Their mother worked from home while caring for her youngest son. "It was impossible for us to go to school or university. We needed all of us employed just to provide for our basic needs.

"Before my father died he registered our family with the UN in Turkey. He was anxious for us not only to be safe, but to eventually be in a country where we could continue our education and where we could contribute to society in a meaningful way. He wanted us to have a future." Rolkana's voice wavered, but she continued, "He loved reading very much, and had a big library at home. He always said to us, 'Read! You have to read!' He read everything he could. As well as studying anaesthetics, he also studied world history in Beirut. My father used to quote a favourite Kurdish poet, Cigerxwîn: *Without learning there can be no progress.*

"My father also taught us to value our Kurdish identity, but at the same time to study and understand other beliefs, cultural practices, and religions... He taught us to be inclusive of others, and to make decisions based on our own convictions. For example, one day in the fourth grade I decided that I would start to wear the *hijab*. My father just said, 'You must try it for yourself and decide if you think it is right for you or not.'

"One-and-a-half years after our UN interview, we were accepted by Norway. Immigrating to a new country is difficult, but I believe my father helped to equip us for this. We were prepared to work and study hard, and for the diversity we have encountered, thanks to his teaching and example. For many coming from Syria, it is very difficult to be here. For instance, the way men and women mix together, and the differences in gender roles, can be quite challenging for people to accept.

"I like to study new languages, and to know what is happening in the world. I want to finish an engineering degree, and my sister Nazli wants to study medicine and work in anaesthetics like our father. Now our family of six are all studying the Norwegian language. We have lost some years because of the war, so we are all working hard to catch up. I need to master academic-level Norwegian before I can apply for university.

"Sometimes I feel like we are in a dream, I am still in shock over what has happened. I often look around, and say to myself, 'Where am I?' It is good here. I feel safe. I have opportunities and the people are kind, but it doesn't feel like home.

"I miss everything about life in Aleppo: family, friends, the crowds of people, my university... our home... the chaos of city life, the noise of cars, people speaking Kurdish... and the smell of jasmine in the evening. I hope I can go back one day... not just to visit, but to stay."

As I trudged back through the snow to my car, I reflected on how this resilient and warm-hearted family has honoured the memory of an extraordinary husband and father in their traumatic passage from Syria and their current re-settlement.

Her many losses and the uncertainty of her future continue to worry Rolkana; she remains separated from her fiancé, who was granted refugee status in Germany. However, with the support of her family and the legacy of her devoted father, she continues to push forward.

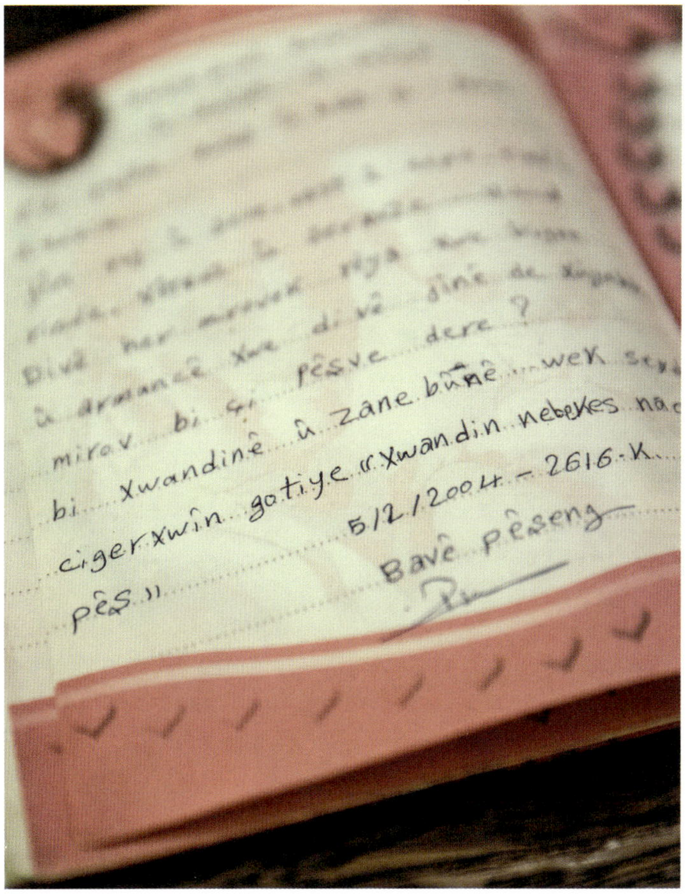

My dear daughter, beloved and precious, I wish you good and sweet days. Life is day and night, right and left, people who love good, and people who love what is evil. Each person should choose his way and deliberately decide his ambition. How can a person progress? With study and knowledge, just as Sayid Cigerxwîn has said, "Study does not leave anyone behind."

A letter to Rolkana from her father

SABANEKH

(savoury lemon minced meat with spinach)

This deep green, flavoursome, and nutritious dish is delicious and so simple to make. Rolkana's family serves *sabanekh* alongside a bowl of white rice and a mountain of *tabbouleh* laced with pomegranate seeds. We crush lemons over our bowls before sharing the meal together.

Serves: 4

INGREDIENTS:

2 tablespoons olive oil

500g (1 lb 2 oz) minced beef or lamb

1 clove crushed fresh garlic

1 large onion, finely diced

1kg (2 lb 3 oz) spinach, rinsed and finely chopped (stems may be removed)

salt and pepper

1 lemon, quartered

1 teaspoon sumac (ground), to garnish

optional garnish: ¼ cup chopped fresh coriander (cilantro)

METHOD:

Heat the olive oil in large saucepan over medium heat. Add the minced meat and cook until browned, breaking it up into small pieces as it cooks. Add the onion and garlic, and fry for 5 minutes.

Add the spinach, one cup at a time. When one cup softens and reduces in size, add the next cup, and so on until all the spinach is added. Season to taste with salt and pepper. Cover and cook on low heat for 10 - 15 minutes.

Check the liquid content after 5 minutes as the spinach cooks down. If the *sabanekh* is very wet, increase the heat a little to help evaporate the excess moisture. When the liquid has gone, the dish is ready. Sprinkle with lemon juice and sumac. Serve with a side of rice and *tabbouleh*.

Greco-Roman ruins, Jerash, Jordan.

Tea and *argilah*, at a downtown café, Amman.

LUBNA home: Damascus, Syria far from home since 2012

لبنى

STORY SALLY BATHGATE | **PHOTOGRAPHY** WILMA STEENBEEK

"I feel like exploding... like there's a volcano inside."

Our hands were full of brightly coloured ribbons. Lubna's two little sons jumped and rolled around on the mattress next to us. Lubna had been decorating hand towels as gifts for people in Australia who have been providing her family with much needed assistance. She was eager to know each person's favourite colours, to make the gifts as personal as she could. She braided and hand stitched the ribbon into flowers and appliquéd the designs onto the towels. Then we put the ribbons away.

"I feel like exploding," she told me, "like there's a volcano inside."

She began to speak of the pressures that were mounting in her life.

She worried for her husband. "My husband is always sick," she said. "I take him to the doctors, but even now we do not know the cause of the disease. He has already had several operations, and we hope he gets better. But since my husband is sick, we sometimes can't even pay the rent; we wait for other people to help us."

She also worried about her sons. She explained, "My sons are not very happy. I don't buy them the things they ask for, I can't offer them new or lovely clothes, I can't buy them toys like other children and I can't take them to play centres. I take them once a month to the public garden, buy them candy, and return back to home. I want to put my son in school, but I can't afford it."

But her greatest worry was for her brother, Mohammed. Her voice faltered as she began to tell me about him, and she wept.

Samir, Lubna's husband, continued for her. "Mohammed used to work in Jordan to try to support his family," he said. "He was only seventeen years old. Sometimes he would work, and he wouldn't get any money from his employer. Since Syrians are not supposed to work, he could do nothing about it. Then one time, the government labour office found out he was working and threatened to return him to Syria. He became so angry, he decided to leave Jordan. We think he went to Turkey, but we don't know where he's gone. That was about a year ago. We haven't heard anything."

They both fell silent. We had all heard the stories of men, women, and children drowning as they attempted to cross by sea from Turkey to Greece. The possibility hung over us, but was not uttered.

A few weeks later, we visit the family again. Lubna has prepared a big feast of chicken, rice, and stuffed vine leaves. She looks brighter, and there is good news: Mohammed has finally made contact and is safe in Germany. Though Samir and Lubna know little else at this stage, the fresh contact has restored some hope.

She shows me the progress of the hand towels. I admire the intricate flowers and adornments — even more, her ability to make and give at a time of such difficulty.

FATTOUSH

(salad with fried bread)

When asked about her favourite salad, Lubna confesses she loves *tabbouleh* the most. But she always wants to know what her guests prefer. If the children like fries, she makes fries. If her friend says she likes *fattoush*, she makes *fattoush*. Feel free to substitute other seasonal salad ingredients as you prefer — it is the bread that makes this salad stand out!

Serves: 6 as a side

INGREDIENTS:

1 flatbread, cut into pieces (recipe p. 142)

60ml (2 fl oz or ⅓ cup) oil, for frying

6 cos (romaine) lettuce leaves, shredded

1 medium-sized cucumber, cut in small chunks

2 tomatoes, cut in small cubes

60g (2 oz or ½ cup) spring onions (scallions), chopped

3 tablespoons flat-leaf parsley, finely chopped

3 tablespoons mint, chopped

155g (5 oz or 1 cup) green capsicum (pepper), chopped

SALAD DRESSING

1 garlic clove, crushed or minced

125ml (4 fl oz or ½ cup) lemon juice

125ml (4 fl oz or ½ cup) olive oil

salt and freshly ground black pepper, to taste

METHOD:

Fry the bread squares in the oil in batches, over low heat. When golden, remove with a slotted spoon to a plate lined with paper towel, to soak up excess oil. Set aside.

Combine the remaining salad ingredients in a large salad bowl.

Mix the salad dressing ingredients and beat thoroughly with a fork. Pour the dressing over the salad, add the bread, toss well and serve.

HUMMUS

(chickpea, tahini and garlic dip)

Hummus, *ful* and *felafal*, served with freshly made flatbreads, are the everyday breakfast of families like Lubna's. Just about every neighbourhood in the Middle East has a little shop that prepares vats of *hummus* and *ful* — a fava bean dip, and *felafal*. It's a bargain breakfast, the quality of which you will rarely taste elsewhere. Many families simply send someone to the shop with the family serving dishes to collect breakfast. The secret to a creamy *hummus* is to separate the chickpeas from their skins. This applies even when you use prepared chickpeas from a can.

Serves: 4 - 6 as an appetiser

INGREDIENTS:

250g (9 oz or 1 cup) dried chickpeas (or 1 can of chickpeas)

1 ½ teaspoons salt

90g (3 oz or ⅓ cup) tahini

125ml (4 fl oz or ½ cup) lemon juice

2 garlic cloves, crushed

FOR SERVING

olive oil, for drizzling

flat-leaf parsley, chopped

paprika or cayenne pepper, for sprinkling

METHOD:

The day before, rinse the chickpeas well and cover with 750ml (25 fl oz or 3 cups) of water. Soak overnight.

Place the chickpeas and soaking water in a saucepan over medium-high heat. Bring to a boil, then reduce the heat and simmer for 2 hours.

Add 1 teaspoon of the salt and cook for a further hour, or until the chickpeas are very tender. Drain, reserving some of the cooking liquid and 1 tablespoon of the chickpeas. As the chickpeas cook, skim off any loose skins. When the chickpeas are cooked, or if using canned chickpeas, soak them in cool water and gently rub them between the palms of your hands to loosen and remove the skins.

Add the soaked chickpeas to a blender or food processor with the remaining ingredients, holding back some lemon juice and salt to adjust the flavour. Blend or process until thick and smooth.

Adjust the flavour and consistency with lemon juice or cooking liquid and add more salt if necessary. Spread in a shallow serving bowl, swirling it with the back of a spoon.

Serve drizzled with olive oil and garnished with the reserved chickpeas, chopped parsley, and a sprinkling of paprika or cayenne pepper.

LOOJEEN

home: Homs, Syria
far from home since 2013

لوجين

STORY NICOLE LAVEZZARI | **PHOTOGRAPHY** KATRINA FLETT GULBRANDSEN

"That's it. When a man is taken, he doesn't return."

The room bustles with the conversation and laughter of fifteen women who gather together to do craft work as part of a refugee-aid project. Plastic bags overflow with brightly coloured yarn, filling the centre of the crowded room. Piles of newly knitted striped sweaters, winter hats, and crocheted blankets line the walls. Women compare handiwork, correcting, inspiring and creating. Needles click; phones ring. Loojeen, who is usually quiet, is especially reserved. Today it is her turn to tell her story, one she has dreaded sharing since she joined the group. As Loojeen begins to speak, the room grows still.

"One night government forces raided the house where my family and I were staying," she says. "My husband's relatives were there along with my husband and three children. One of my children was hiding in a blanket, while the other two hid behind me. Almost immediately, one by one, the soldiers began to slaughter my husband's relatives. When they reached my husband, they tied him up and started beating him, asking him all kinds of questions and making many accusations. I had to answer for him because he couldn't speak. Then they turned to me and shoved a gun in my mouth, all the way to my throat, and threatened to shoot. At that point, my son, who was hiding behind me, passed out. When the soldiers saw this, one of the men said, 'Don't shoot, for the kids' sake.' Then they grabbed my husband and left.

"I thought, 'That's it. When a man is taken, he doesn't return.'

"Half an hour later my husband did return, almost unrecognisable from the beating he had endured. We gathered then and there as a family and prayed. And when the opportunity arose later that night, we fled."

As Loojeen tells her story, tears well up in her eyes and in the eyes of every woman in the room. They each have their own painful story, but in that moment, they grieve with her and share her burden.

In the weeks that follow, there is a change in Loojeen. It has been a relief for her to tell her story. She is freer, opening up – unfurling paper-thin wings, engaging more in the friendly commotion of the group.

"After I shared my story and saw how everyone supported me, I felt more comfortable within the gathering," she says. "After one group is finished, I start looking forward to the next one. Life as a refugee is difficult, but I am so thankful that I have people that I can share my hardships with. I can't talk about these things in my home, and so before, I felt very alone. Now I know that I am not."

SHISHBARAK

(lamb dumplings in yoghurt sauce)

The humble dumpling: stuffed with delicious ground meat and local seasoning and served in broth or sauce, these parcels of flavour are found in various expressions throughout Eurasia — from the pork dumpling soups of East Asia through to tortellini and ravioli in Italy. In the Middle East we find lamb-filled dumplings served in yoghurt, an adaptation well fitting ingredients more commonly found and used in this region. Loojeen shares her delectable version of *shishbarak* with us here.

Serves: 4 - 6

INGREDIENTS:

DOUGH

600g (1 lb 5 oz or 4 ½ cups) of plain (all-purpose) flour

1 teaspoon salt

370ml (13 fl oz or 1 ½ cups) water

FILLING

olive oil

2 small onions, finely chopped

500g (1 lb 2 oz) finely minced lamb

40g (1 ½ oz or ¼ cup) pine nuts

1 teaspoon ground black pepper

salt, to taste

YOGHURT SAUCE

1.25kg (2 lb 12 oz or 5 cups) plain yoghurt

500ml (17 fl oz or 2 cups) water

1 egg white, lightly beaten

½ teaspoon salt

2 garlic cloves, crushed

1 teaspoon dried crushed mint

½ teaspoon dried crushed coriander (cilantro)

METHOD:

Mix the flour, salt, and water in a food processor (or knead by hand), until the dough is smooth and soft, adding a little extra flour if needed. Cover with cling film and leave to rest at room temperature for 20 minutes.

Meanwhile, fry the onions gently in a generous splash of olive oil for 10 minutes. Add the lamb and fry for a further 5 minutes while stirring to break down the mince and prevent it from clumping. Stir in the pine nuts, and salt and pepper to taste. Cook for a further 5 minutes. Remove from the heat and allow to cool slightly.

Preheat the oven to 180°C (350°F/Gas 4).

Roll out the dough on a lightly floured surface to a thickness of about ½cm (⅛ inch). Using a small cookie cutter, cut the dough into 5cm (2-inch) rounds.

Place 1 teaspoon of filling in the centre of each round and fold the dough over. Press the edges to seal. Pull the edges around and press the two points together, then flatten the sides to a hat or tortellini shape.

(Surplus dumplings can be frozen for future use. Lay the dumplings on a flour-dusted tray in the freezer for 2 hours, then transfer them to zip-lock bags.)

Place the dumplings on a greased baking tray and bake in the preheated oven for 10 - 15 minutes or until golden. It is important to cook the dumplings so that they will hold together in the sauce.

Meanwhile, to make the yoghurt sauce, place the yoghurt, water, egg white, and salt in a large, heavy-based saucepan. Over medium-low heat, stir gently and constantly in the same direction to prevent curdling. When the mixture reaches a boil, turn the heat to low, and add the dumplings. Stir gently until the dumplings are heated through.

To finish, add the garlic, mint, and coriander, and stir. Serve in deep bowls with a side of rice, if desired.

Amman, Jordan.

OLIVE OIL SOAP sabun zeyt i zeytoun

with Menahi and a Syrian handicraft group, Jordan

Start a conversation about olive oil soap with almost any Arab woman, especially if she is over forty: you will engage her in a special way. Olive oil soap has thousand-year-old roots in the Levant and a well-deserved reputation abroad. Tradition holds that Queen Elizabeth I ordered it from Nablus and used it to keep her skin pristine. Simple and earthy, olive oil soap lathers gently and leaves skin firm and lightly scented.

My dear friend Menahi, whose father escaped the Armenian genocide as a boy and settled in Jordan, grew up making soap in her mother's ancestral village, Taybeh. She and her female family members would prepare their soap in a big pot outside, over an open fire. As they stirred the olive oil, lye, and water to readiness, they would exchange stories and wisdom in conversations that would continue through the day's other tasks: soaking rice, cooking meals, sorting herbs for drying. Menahi, now in her seventies, still swears by olive oil soap for household washing, skin and hair care. She has only ever used olive oil soap as her shampoo throughout her life. Convinced nothing can make one's hair and skin healthy the way olive oil soap does, she runs one of her smooth hands over the other as she discusses the best way to make it.

"I make olive oil soap out of the oil we produce from our olives the same way my mother did. I like that it is pure; you don't know what they put in soap today! Sometimes I make the traditional pure olive oil soap, like my mother and Palestinian father-in-law did. But sometimes I now add coconut oil and sometimes I take rosemary, lavender, or bay leaves from the garden, dry them, and then add them to the soap; it smells wonderful!"

When we make olive oil soap in a crowded kitchen with a Syrian women's craft group, the women watch attentively, wanting to master this ancient art with roots deep in their own culture. Aleppo soap, a striking green soap stamped with curling Arabic lettering, is recognised and appreciated in Syria and throughout the world. We use a food scale, wooden spoons, and glass jam jars. Taking our three ingredients of water, lye from the *souk*, and olive oil produced from local trees, we mix carefully — eyes wide at the threat of noxious fumes or an explosion should water be added to lye instead of the reverse. We wear gloves and pay close attention, assigning a new stirrer every few minutes as we prepare moulds, pour coffee, and gossip about a recent wedding.

"Is it ready now?" the women strain to see inside the slow cooker in which we've heated our mixture. "Not firm enough... No, too firm!" Opinions and gentle arguments fly over the craned heads. When the shiny green soap appears sticky and lumpy, we all rush to scoop it into waiting moulds. A *"bismillah"* slips out of one mouth in a whisper as we wish the process success. The moulds filled, we sigh as our work is completed for the night. We will leave the moulds to rest for at least a few days as the soap hardens, before cutting it into bars. Months later, the soap will be aged to perfection, lathering richly and subtly scented. One woman washes the dishes in the sink using the newly made soap residue to clean utensils; she nods approval of the lather as the water sloshes about.

With our soap curing, we move on to more important things — the evening ends in a dance party, scarves tied around our hips and laughter bathing our conversation.

As the night grows late, the zip of *abayahs* and calls of good night usher us into the cool outside air. We part ways for home.

STORY KELLY FOWLER | **PHOTOGRAPHY** KATRINA FLETT GULBRANDSEN

صابون
أبو سعد
النابلسي
الصابون النابلسي الفاخر

Blackberry
Curcuma كركم

MAKE IT:

Cold process olive oil soap

Varieties:
pure olive
lemon & mint
Arabic coffee & cardamom
orange blossom & poppy seed

YOU WILL NEED:

1kg olive oil

250g coconut oil (adding coconut oil decreases the required curing time, and creates a smoother lather)

172g lye (sodium hydroxide)

450ml water

VARIATIONS:
lemon & mint — 12.5g spearmint and 12.5g lemon essential oils, with 2 tablespoons of dried, crushed mint leaves and 2 tablespoons of grated and dried lemon rind, for decorating the soap

Arabic coffee & cardamom — 6.5g cardamom essential oil, with 2 tablespoons of cardamom powder and 1 tablespoon of used coffee grounds

orange blossom & poppy seed — 12.5g neroli (orange blossom) essential oil, with 1 tablespoon of poppy seeds and 2 tablespoons of turmeric powder

Note: The above quantities will suffice to infuse half a batch of plain soap — double these measurements if you would like to make a full batch of one type.

EQUIPMENT:

500ml measuring jug for water

electronic kitchen scales (accuracy is important)

3L stainless steel saucepan (to heat oils)

1L tempered glass jug or bowl (for water and lye mixture)

2 food thermometers

wooden or plastic spoon

stick blender

moulds: loaf tins, muffin trays, ice block trays, milk cartons, or any plastic or silicone container

baking paper or muffin papers

plastic wrap

old towel

sharp knife or thin wire

drying rack

olive oil soap continued on next page

SAFETY TIPS:

Wear gloves, goggles, long sleeves, and a mask. Lye is caustic. It can eat holes in fabric and burn your skin.

Add lye to water, never add water to lye (this can cause an explosion).

Work in a well-ventilated room.

Use equipment that will not be used for cooking.

Stainless steel, tempered glass and enamel are good choices for mixing bowls.

Protect your work surface with newspaper or an old tablecloth.

PROCESS:

1. Prepare and set out moulds (2 paper-lined loaf tins or equivalent).
2. Put on safety equipment.
3. Measure and weigh all ingredients (oil, lye, and water), placing the oils (olive and coconut) into the large saucepan, and the water into the heat resistant jug/bowl.
4. Carefully pour the lye (172g) into the water (450ml) and stir gently and thoroughly until fully dissolved. Be aware that fumes will emanate from the mixture as it heats up.

Note: Good ventilation is essential. For this part of the process you may want to place the jug in the kitchen sink in the event of spillage. Attach the first thermometer to the side of the jug. The mixture will heat rapidly and then start to cool.

5. Clip the second thermometer onto the side of the saucepan containing the oils. Place on low heat on the stove. Slowly heat oils to 50°C (122°F).
6. Monitor the temperatures of your lye-water solution and your oil mixture. When the lye solution and the melted oils reach approximately the same temperature — 50°C (122°F), slowly pour the solution into the oils, being careful not to let it splash.
7. Using the stick blender, blend the oil and lye mixture for approximately 5 - 10 minutes, until the mixture reaches trace. Trace is the sign you look for that the soap has become stable and is ready to be poured into a mould. When you reach trace, slight ripples will form on the surface and remain there (see photo below). The mixture should be thick, but pourable.

Note: Work carefully, remembering that the soap is still caustic at this stage, and try not to overheat your blender.

8. If you want to make pure olive soap, your soap mixture is now ready to be poured into prepared moulds. If you have access to dried lavender or rosemary, like Menahi, you could try crumbling a handful and adding it now. If you would like to try some of our variations, now add them to the soap mixture, and stir thoroughly to combine. We suggest dividing the mixture in half, and trying two variations at a time. The amounts of additives (per half mixture) are given in the variations list.
9. Pour the mixture into the moulds and cover with plastic wrap. Wrap the covered moulds in an old towel. This will keep in the residual heat and start the saponification process. Saponification occurs when the base ingredients become soap.
10. Approximately 15 hours later, carefully release the soap from the mould, and cut it into whatever shaped bars you desire with a sharp knife or taut wire.
11. Place the soaps on a drying rack. Turn the soaps over every day for a couple of weeks, to allow them to dry out evenly. Leave soaps for about 6 weeks to cure before using them. The drier they are when you use them, the longer they last and the better they will be!

"Many years ago, olive oil soap making was a village event. Each year at the same time, the young women would come together to make soap for the whole village. The soap making took place outside, using huge vats to mix the lye-water and oil. While heating the soap mixture, a single gold coin was tossed into the vat. When the mixture had thickened, it was poured into ceramic moulds. The bars of soap were then cut and stored until cured. After the soap had cured for some months, the young women would come back together to divide the soap amongst their families. It was believed that the young woman who found the gold coin in her soap would be blessed. She was destined to be the next bride in the village!"

Menahi

UM MOHAMMED

home: Homs, Syria
far from home since 2013

أم محمد

STORY NICOLE LAVEZZARI | **PHOTOGRAPHY** KATRINA FLETT GULBRANDSEN

"Our faith has given us patience — after trouble there is provision."

Um Mohammed smiles kindly. Her presence is calming, and though she has been burdened by much grief and pain, she lends her strength to other women who have suffered similar losses back in Syria.

As she shares her story, she weeps, yet her smile remains. She is like a tree that can withstand storms because its roots go down deep.

"We moved from place to place, and at each one there was trouble — fighting and bombing. After my brother was killed, we stayed in one place... moving was dangerous. We stayed in my uncle's village, just the women. The men were not allowed out of Homs. At the checkpoints the authorities would see Baba Amr, Homs on the ID cards and our men would be arrested. My son and two of my nephews were taken that way; they took them to a building and gunned them down.

"The army killed around one hundred and fifty boys during that time. The boys hadn't done anything. My son was only sixteen. He didn't know anything. He was still in school."

Soon after, Um Mohammed's husband began fighting for the Free Syrian Army. He was killed. Um Mohammed, worried that the family would suffer retaliation for her husband's part in the war, decided she must flee the country. She now lives in Jordan as a widow, raising her remaining children amongst other Syrian refugees.

"Our lives are completely changed here, but we have to adapt. Life was happy. Now we don't feel any sweetness in life. Many people we love have died, but we must keep going. Life doesn't stop. Hopefully we can make it better for our children."

As a widow and a refugee, she has experienced both assistance and exploitation. NGOs have provided for some of her family's basic needs, however, to receive UN aid outside a camp setting, refugees need a local sponsor, which Um Mohammed has been unable to secure. (Many refugees choose to live outside of the camps due to poor living conditions and security risks.) Without UN aid, Um Mohammed supports her family by knitting for a small charity.

Despite all of her suffering, Um Mohammed's faith, the source of her deep-rooted resilience, sustains her. "Islam is about forgiveness and love. It is a religion of peace and is full of goodness, not evil. Islam gives us patience and we know that goodness will triumph over evil. This motivates us in our lives, and it gives us hope.

"Our faith has given us patience — after trouble there is provision. We pray many prayers to help us, and I recite *Surah Yaseen* and *Surah al Baqarah* from the Quran. There are many stories where God brings good out of hardship.

"Alhamdulillah."

KIBBEH

(stuffed minced lamb and burghul balls)

This dish is another labour of love, especially for households without a food processor. In that case, the meat for the *kibbeh* casing is often a lean cut of lamb from the butcher, ground finely with the butcher shop meat grinder. At home it is then pounded by hand with the burghul (bulgur), onion, and spices, using a mortar and pestle. For Arab women like Um Mohammed, domestic life is far from sedentary!

Serves: 6

INGREDIENTS:

KIBBEH CASING

600g (1 lb 5 oz or 3 cups) burghul (bulgur)

1kg (2 lb 3 oz) minced lean lamb

1 large onion, chopped

3 teaspoons salt

1 teaspoon freshly ground black pepper

1 teaspoon ground allspice

125ml (4 fl oz or ½ cup) iced water or ice chips

FILLING

60g (2 oz or ¼ cup) ghee or oil

2 onions, finely diced

40g (1 ½ oz or ¼ cup) pine nuts

250g (9 oz) minced lamb or beef

salt and pepper, to taste

¼ teaspoon ground cinnamon

oil, for brushing

METHOD:

FOR THE CASING:

Place the burghul in a bowl, cover with cold water and leave to soak for 10 minutes. Drain in a sieve and press with the back of a spoon to remove as much moisture as possible. Tip into a flat dish, spread out, and chill for 1 - 2 hours.

Using a food processor, process the onion to a thick liquid. In a large bowl, combine the meat with the onion, salt and pepper, allspice and burghul. Process this mixture in small batches, adding a tablespoon of iced water or ice chips to each lot. Knead the processed mixture by hand. Cover and chill until required.

FOR THE FILLING:

Heat the ghee or oil in a frypan and gently fry the onion for 3 minutes. Add the pine nuts and fry until the nuts are golden brown.

Increase the heat and add the meat. Cook, stirring occasionally, until the juices evaporate and the meat begins to brown. Remove from the heat and add the salt, pepper, and cinnamon.

Preheat the oven to 180°C (350°F/Gas 4).

Shape lumps of chilled *kibbeh* casing mixture into balls about the size of ping pong balls. Dip your hands in cold water, roll a ball of *kibbeh* casing in your palms until smooth, then make a hole in the ball with your index finger. Work your finger around the hole until you have a shell of even thickness.

Fill the hole with the filling mixture and close the opening. Moisten with cold water to seal well. If any breaks appear in the shell, close them with wet fingers.

Complete the shape to resemble a football with pointed ends. Place side by side in a greased baking dish and brush well with oil. Bake for 20 - 25 minutes, uncovered.

Serve hot or cold with salads, yoghurt, and flatbread.

WESAM

home: Homs, Syria
far from home since 2013

وسام

STORY TARYN LAMMI & NICOLE LAVEZZARI | **PHOTOGRAPHY** KATRINA FLETT GULBRANDSEN

"I don't care about the money. All I want is to get out of here."

Wesam motions for us to take a seat on her couch as she moves about the house. She also has a bed and an automatic washing machine. This, compared to the houses of other refugees — where the mattresses on the floor are used for both sitting and sleeping, and where a washing machine of any kind would be a luxury — is one of the better-furnished temporary houses we've seen. But as she tells her story, it is clear she has known both poverty and wealth, and that her wealth potentially saved her life.

"I grew up living in a small house. My family was poor, but those were the best days. After high school, I got married and had four children. It was during my fourth pregnancy that the war started. When my due date was near, I insisted on leaving for the hospital early, because it was impossible to predict when the streets would be open. When my mother and I arrived at the hospital, there was a lot of fighting and bombs dropping. After giving birth, I had to stay a while longer, waiting for it to be safe enough to leave.

"Near the end of our time in Syria, the kids and I were staying with my mother-in-law. One winter night, someone knocked on the door. It was the Free Syrian Army, telling us, 'You need to leave. *Alawites* are coming.' The government forces were coming and killing everyone in their houses.

"They took us to a safe place, but there were no telephones and I couldn't get in contact with my husband. He had no idea that we were leaving. It was more than a day before I was able to get hold of him. Though it was dangerous, *Alhamdulillah*, my husband and brother were able to get out.

"After reuniting, we moved to Damascus. I wanted to go to Jordan, but my husband didn't want to leave. Damascus was supposed to be safer, especially since we still had some money left. But after a particularly bad bombing, I had had enough. There was no way I wanted to stay in Syria! I confronted my husband, 'Look! Nowhere is safe here!' However, even after the bomb, he was still not convinced we were to leave. Then my husband received tragic news that a close friend of his had been killed in Al-Hameh. After that he agreed to leave.

"We tried leaving through the airport three times, but the Syrian government would not let us. We explained our situation to a soldier living above us, hoping he could offer us some help.

'I will make sure you get out,' he told us. 'But it will cost you.'

'I don't care about the money,' I thought. 'All I want is to get out of here.'

"When the time came, the soldier guided us through the airport. He took our $300 and put it in our passports. He walked away but stayed on the phone with my husband so he could give us further instructions. 'Give your passports with the money to that man, then back away and sit down.' We did. Our bribe was accepted and we were able to leave.

"After nearly a year-and-a-half of hardships and unease, we were able to leave our home — Syria — and began a new life with different hardships and unease in Jordan."

Woman serving *duwali* at a produce market, Amman.

DUWALI

(stuffed grapevine leaves)

Few things confer as much honour upon a visitor as being offered freshly made *duwali*. Many of the Syrian women we met were eager to include this dish as their recipe for the book. These individually wrapped parcels of meat and rice are time-consuming to make, but for Wesam the labour required is a source of pride, especially if friends or family join in the making and eating. This recipe presents Wesam's classic version of *duwali*. Once you get rolling, the possible variations of fillings and flavourings are endless.

Serves: 8 (as a side or appetiser)

INGREDIENTS:

60 fresh vine leaves, or 375g (13 oz) preserved vine leaves — drained weight

2 tablespoons lemon juice for cooking, plus 2 tablespoons to garnish before serving

2 tablespoons butter or ghee

1 bulb of garlic, separated into cloves

500ml (17 fl oz or 2 cups) water or chicken stock

FILLING

2 tablespoons oil

1 onion, finely chopped

750g (1 lb 10 oz) minced meat (lamb or beef), raw

110g (3 ¾ oz or ½ cup) short-grain rice (uncooked)

salt and pepper, to taste

METHOD:

If working with fresh vine leaves, rinse the leaves in cold water and then add them to a saucepan of boiling water, 20 at a time, and boil for 2 minutes. Remove to a pot of cold water, then drain in a colander. If using preserved vine leaves, rinse and drain them in a colander.

To make the filling, fry the onion gently in oil until soft. Add the onion to a bowl with the other filling ingredients and mix.

Open the leaves and place them shiny side down on your work surface. Remove any stems. Place 1 tablespoon of filling near the stem end. Fold the stem end and sides over the filling, then roll up firmly. Repeat. Set aside any damaged leaves to line the cooking pan.

Place 1 tablespoon of butter in a heavy-based saucepan along with the garlic. Cover the butter and garlic with a layer of leaves, then pack in the rolls, closely together, in layers. Sprinkle each layer with lemon juice.

Cover the top layer with the remaining vine leaves, add the remaining butter, and the stock. Place an inverted plate over the rolls so that they keep their shape during cooking. Bring to a boil, then reduce the heat. Simmer gently, covered, for about 1 ½ - 2 hours.

Drain the *duwali* and arrange on a serving dish, sprinkling with lemon juice, if desired.

Downtown Mafraq.

BEDOUIN WOOL WEAVING nasj al suuf

A traditional Bedouin handicraft

It is late afternoon. It's my favourite time of the day to take a long drive through the desert. As we drive the pot-holed highway home, I stare out the window at a barren landscape dotted with woven, black Bedouin tents. The sky is golden and the pale desert-scape looks sleepy and serene after a scorching day. The scene is timeless and ancient, stretching across the deserts of the Middle East and North Africa.

I see a young Bedouin shepherd boy — he is small and wiry. He wears an American baseball cap, stained jeans, and a red and white chequered *keffieh* wrapped loosely around his face. He carries a long staff. Behind him a flock of mottled and matted sheep and goats follow their shepherd home, bleating and forming a billowing dust cloud with hundreds of small hooves. The dust particles get caught up with the desert wind and fly wildly upward for metres into the blue; I can still see the cloud long after the shepherd has disappeared from view.

The Bedouin way of life has been deeply affected by the current conflicts in Syria and Iraq. Many Bedouin, whether settled or nomadic, have been displaced within their countries, and many have sought asylum here in Jordan.

Bedouin use their goat and sheep flocks for meat, milk, and wool production. The coarse wool and hair is used to weave large tents, and other durable household items suitable for a harsh desert life. In some parts of the region, the wool is still hand-sheared, washed and carded, and spun using a small, hand-held, wooden spindle called a *maghazal*.

The spun yarn is then either dyed or left natural — white, cream, grey, brown or black. In the past, vegetable and mineral dyes were used to colour the wool in a range of dark and earthy colours; today it is easier and more economical to use artificial dyes.

Traditionally, Bedouin women would weave the yarn into rugs and tent pieces on simple ground looms made of sticks. These looms could be easily taken apart and relocated when a family moved its tent with the changing season. Today many Bedouin live in towns and villages, and iron vertical looms are more typically used.

Rug making skills once common in the region still exist, but are often not practised. However, thanks to handicraft conservation and income-generating initiatives aimed at benefiting low-income families and refugees, a new generation of weavers are being taught the traditional skills. This core element of Bedouin heritage is being preserved and revitalised.

Rugs are still made in traditional styles and patterns — stripes and geometric designs being the most common. The rugs, carpets, pillows, and bags can be found piled high in small shops in city *souks* or purchased from handicraft centres throughout the region.

STORY & PHOTOGRAPHY KATRINA FLETT GULBRANDSEN.

A traditional wool Bedouin tent, Wadi Rum, Jordan. ABOVE: A Bedouin boy and his flock of sheep. RIGHT: Antique rugs mixed with contemporary designs inspired by the traditional craft, Jordan.

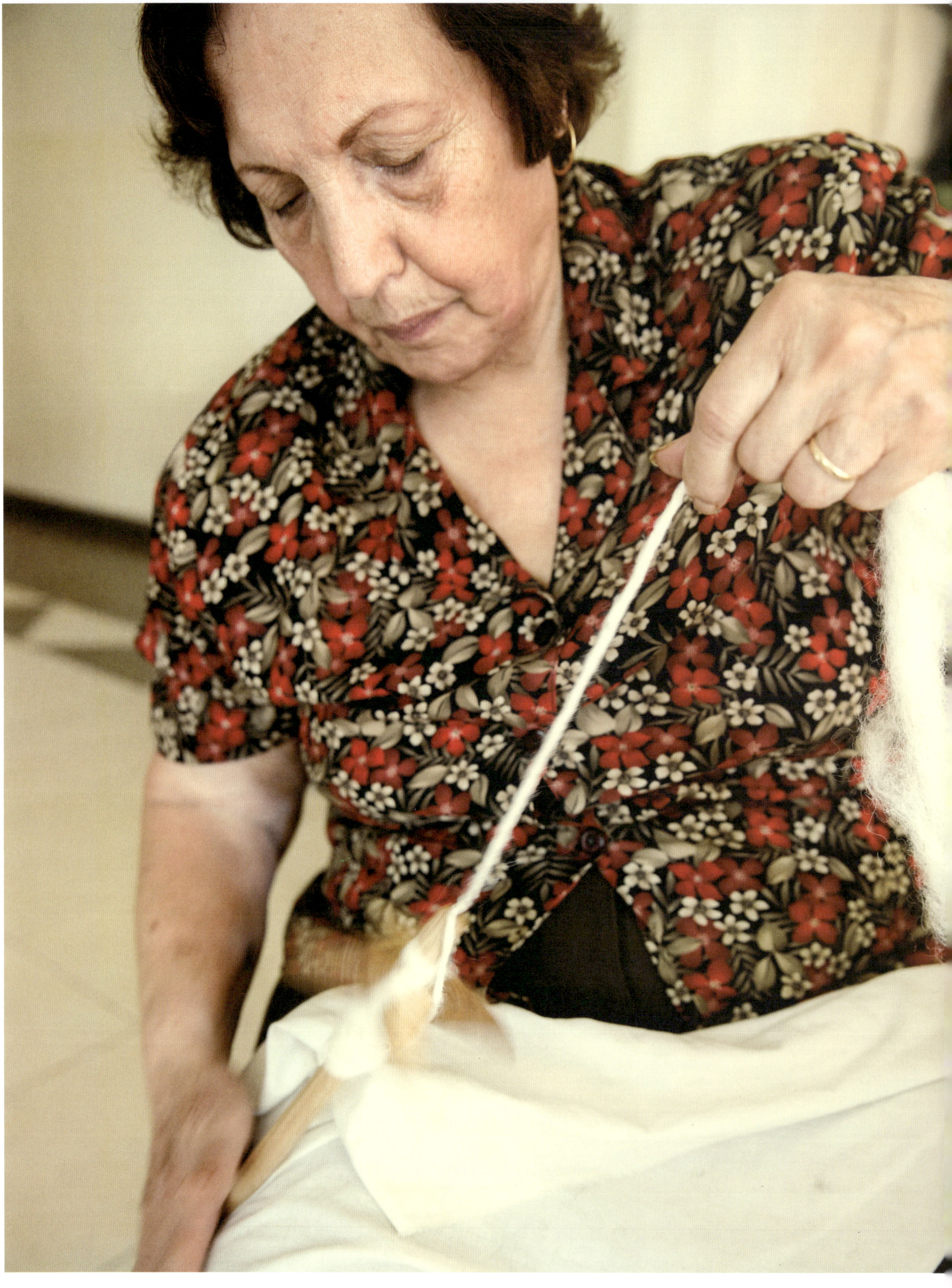

MAKE IT:

Bedouin-style woven wall hanging

To experience the tactile and creative pleasures of weaving on a small scale, make your own Bedouin-inspired wall hanging. Choose natural, dark, and earthy wool colours for a more traditional-looking weaving, or create something in alternate colours to suit your own home. Vary your stripe-width and pattern according to your own inspiration.

LEFT: Menahi demonstrates traditional wool spinning. She learned the craft from her mother, who would spin wool from the family's sheep to knit warm winter socks for her children. ABOVE: The hand-cut *maghazal*, handed down to Menahi by her mother. It is made of olive wood from the family's olive grove and is smooth and shiny from use.

YOU WILL NEED:

a simple hand-held weaving loom — available at craft stores, or make your own with a solid timber picture frame and small nails

balls of wool or other yarn — the colour, ply, and quantity will depend on your own design and the size of your loom

1 ball of crochet cotton or cotton yarn (string)

a fork

a 3 - 5cm wide piece of cardboard the width of your loom

a shed stick — a piece of wooden dowel or a wooden spoon the width of your loom works well (approximately 1 - 2cm in diameter)

scissors

a tapestry needle (with a curved tip)

a hanging rod, approximately the width of your loom (stick or dowel)

weaving continued on next page

PROCESS:

1. Cut a cardboard strip approximately 3 - 5cm wide (depending on the size of your loom) and as long as the width of your loom. This cardboard barrier creates a space for you to tie off the warp threads when you complete your weaving. Set aside for step 4.
2. Warp your loom with the crochet cotton. The warp is the vertical threading that will hold the weaving together. To begin, tie your cotton in a double knot around your loom at the top left corner (or first nail, if you have this type of loom). Bring the cotton through the first top notch. Pull the cotton taut, and guide it into the first notch at the bottom, around and back up to the next top notch. Warp the whole loom in this manner. Tie the cotton to finish through the last notch and secure with a double knot.
3. Check the tension of the warp thread — when you push down on the threads lightly they should bounce back.
4. Weave the cardboard strip through the base of the frame. Your first woven row of weft (the horizontal wool or yarn) will sit against the cardboard.
5. Take your shed stick and weave it through the warp threads (over, under, over, under ...). This stick is used to open up an area (or shed) that the needle can pass through easily. When the row is completed, the shed stick can be pushed to the top of the frame, so the needle can weave back in the opposite direction.
6. Cut a piece of your desired-colour yarn, approximately 1m in length (or a shorter length if it feels more comfortable to work with). If you would like a fringe in a particular colour, make sure you begin with this colour. Thread your needle.
7. To secure your first row of weft, take the tail end of your yarn and weave it by hand through approximately 5 - 8 warp threads, starting from the right bottom corner. Leave approximately 5cm of the tail hanging at the back.
8. To begin your first row of weft (weaving from right to left), take the needle and weave over, under, over, under... until you complete the row, leaving the woven yarn in a gentle arc over the cardboard. Keep the weave loose enough so that at all times, throughout the weaving, the end warp threads remain parallel with the loom sides. This is very important to keep the shape of the weaving uniform.
9. Use your fork to gently push down the yarn — working from the middle, so it sits against the cardboard barrier. Remember to keep it loose!
10. Repeat the process back in the other direction. Use the shed stick for alternate rows to speed up the process.
11. When new yarn is required, leave 5cm of your current yarn to the back of the weaving and bring up the new yarn through the same space, also leaving a tail of approximately 5cm at the back.
12. If you would like to create a fringe, you will need at least 2.5cm of plain weave as a base before starting the fringe. This will allow the fringe to fall evenly.
13. For the fringe, take your base-colour yarn and cut strands at least double the desired length of your fringe. You will use at least 3 strands per fringe knot. Lay the centre of 3 strands over the first two warp threads. Bring each side under and back through the centre of the threads (see picture). To tighten the knot, pull the threads up towards the top of the loom and then down firmly into position on top of your last row of weft. Continue until the end of the row. If you have an extra warp thread, use 3 for your last knot.
14. Continue with plain weaving in your fringe colour to your desired stripe width.
15. At this stage, continue weaving, creating your desired individual pattern.
16. When you complete your weaving, you will need to leave at least 5cm of warp thread at the top. This thread will be used to tie off the weaving and also to pass your hanging rod through. If you have a larger weaving and therefore require a larger rod, you will need to leave more thread.
17. When you have completed your last row, take the yarn through to the back and using the needle, pass it under a few weaves to secure it. Trim any extra yarn.
18. At the bottom of the weaving, slide out the cardboard. Push the fringe out of the way. Cut any double knots used to secure the thread to the loom. Gently take each loop out of the notches, releasing the base of the weaving from the loom.
19. Tie each loop with an over-hand knot. Push the knot firmly up against the first row of weave. If you have a single thread on either end, tie it in with the closest loop.
20. Release and tie the top warp threads in the same manner; however, leave any single end threads loose.
21. Turn over the weaving. Using your needle, pass each loose end thread under a few weaves to secure it. Trim off excess thread. Now do the same with any yarn tails.
22. Trim fringe as desired.
23. Pass hanging rod through the top warp thread loops, keeping all loops sitting in the same direction.
24. Tie some extra yarn to the rod for hanging.

Weaving steps pictured by row, from left to right:
first row: 2; 4 and 5 and 7; 8; 9 **second row:** 10; 10; 12 and 13; 12 and 13 **third row:** 14; 15; 16 and 17; 18 **fourth row:** 18; 19 **fifth row:** 20; 20 **sixth row:** 21; 22 **large image:** 23 and 24

Byzantine ruins of Um al-Jimal, Jordan, near the Syrian border.

Recipe Index

Handicraft index

Arabic glossary

abayah: over-dress worn by women

ahlan wa sahlan: welcome, you are among family, may it go well with you

Alawite: a branch of Shia Islam, mainly practiced in the northwest of Syria

Allah makum: God be with you

al-nakbah: the Catastrophe—the 1948 Arab-Israeli War and Palestinian exodus

Alhamdulillah: praise be to God

argilah: water pipe

atar: apothecary or perfumery

bashoufik badayn: see you later (as addressed to a woman)

bein-na khubbiz u maleh: there is bread and salt between us (idiom for close friendship)

bismillah: a prayerful wish for a successful outcome

boosa: bamboo calligraphy pen

bukra ahla: tomorrow is a better day

Eid al-Adha: holiday at the end of the annual pilgrimage to Mecca

Eid al-Fitr: holiday at end of Ramadan

itfaddali: come/come in

halal: a term commonly applied to food and drinks, if their consumption is permissible according to the Quran

haram: a kind of opposite of halal, something unlawful or forbidden

hijab: head covering for women

iftar: the meal eaten after sundown during Ramadan

inshallah: God willing

keefik: how are you (addressed to a woman)

keffieh: a square cloth traditionally worn on the head by Arab men

niqab: veil worn by some Muslim women, covering all of the face except for the eyes

qunbula: grenade or bomb

rakwah: long-handled coffee pot

Ramadan: the ninth lunar month in the Islamic calendar, during which able adult Muslims usually observe a daytime fast — the fast commemorates the revelation of the Quran to the prophet Mohammed

saha: to your health

shay: tea

Shia: the second largest sect of Islam, which regards Ali, the son-in-law of Mohammed, as the legitimate subsequent leader of Islam, disregarding the three caliphs who succeeded him

shukran habibti: thank you, my dear (addressed to a woman)

soba: heater

souk: market

Sunni: the largest sect of Islam, which regards the first four caliphs as legitimate successors of Mohammed, and focuses on the importance of the *sunna* — the recorded words and acts of Mohammed

surat al baqara: a chapter of the Quran entitled "The Cow"

surat yaseen: a chapter of the Quran entitled "Yaseen"

tabi: decoratively carved biscuit mould

Quran: believed to be the word of God as revealed to Mohammed by the angel Gabriel, recorded in Arabic

zafeh: a musical parade at the beginning of a wedding, which may include drums, pipes, horns, flaming swords, belly dancers